500

student meals

500

student meals

the only student cookbook you'll ever need

Deborah Gray

APPLE

A QUINTET BOOK

First published 2015 in the UK by
Apple Press
74-77 White Lion Street
London N1 9PF
United Kingdom

www.apple-press.com

ISBN: 978-1-84543-622-3
QTT.FHSM

Conceived, designed, and produced by:
Quintet Publishing Limited
4th Floor, Sheridan House
114–116 Western Road
Hove, East Sussex
BN3 1DD
UK

Food Stylist: Valentina Harris
Photographer: Ian Garlick
Designer: Tania Gomes
Art Director: Michael Charles
Editorial Assistant: Ella Lines
Publishing Assistant: Alice Sambrook
Editorial Director: Emma Bastow
Publisher: Mark Searle

10 9 8 7 6 5 4 3 2 1

Printed in China by 1010 Printing International Ltd.

contents

introduction

This book is written with you, the hungry and budget-strapped student, in mind. The recipes have been simplified to ensure success and reduce the ingredients you need to buy – but not at the cost of taste! Follow the instructions and you'll be surprised at how easy it is to produce delicious food even if you're not an experienced cook. The book presumes you have only one shelf in the cupboard and in the fridge and uses a limited palette of ingredients. Most recipes only use one burner on the cooker at a time because everyone always seems to cook at once, no matter what time you choose to eat! Cooking is an art, not a science, and most recipes are adaptable. Use what you have to hand or feel like eating, and substitute your favoured ingredients for those less appealing to you. Most importantly, have fun in the kitchen!

living on a budget

Shopping wisely and using everything we buy, including leftovers, avoids wasting money and makes sound environmental sense. It's a good idea to plan your meals and shop with the menu for a few days in mind. Many of the recipes in this book draw from a range of ingredients, so if you buy a jar of roasted red peppers, for instance, you'll find several ways to use them up without eating the same meal over and over. To minimise waste, be aware of what needs to be used up and work your menu plan around that before shopping for more perishables. You'll soon get the hang of thinking up something to make with the multiple vegetable bits in the fridge – perhaps a soup, or buy a few prawns and make a stirfry.

Avoid the trap of false bargains that supermarkets offer to entice us to buy more. Bulk buying is only a good deal if you use it all up. Check the best-by dates to ensure you'll have time to use it. Also, try shopping late in the day to pick up bargains. But be sensible – it's great to buy one piece of fish for next to nothing, but buying four that end up smelling in the fridge or hiding in the freezer is a false economy. Be realistic about your eating capacity.

Buy food in markets and local and ethnic shops to find seasonal produce at good prices and avoid the supermarket tyranny of the perfectly formed carrot and plastic packaging. Smaller suppliers are often happy to sell you smaller quantities, and often know their produce and how to cook it, so can offer cooking tips. But if you do shop at supermarkets, buy own brands rather than premium products, especially on items such as canned tomatoes and beans. And never shop when you are hungry!

healthy eating

A student lifestyle isn't conducive to healthy eating – it's all too easy to rely on fast food and restaurant meals with friends, or to eat quick snacks and ready meals high in salt, sugar and saturated fats. Be vigilant and balance out the good with the bad. Most of the recipes in this book are sensible but some are unhealthy too, like the chocolate brownies, which are high in sugar and fat. Ensure you don't make them every day, and that you eat your fair share of healthy dishes. Healthy eating advice changes, but the constants are outlined here.

The golden rules

Eat and drink the correct amount of food you need to sustain your lifestyle. Eating too much will cause you to put on weight; conversely, if you eat and drink too little, you'll lose weight. The average man needs around 2,500 calories a day. The average woman needs 2,000 calories. Most people eat more calories than they need and most people are not average!

Eat a wide range of foods to give you a balanced diet so your body receives all the nutrients it needs. Eating a range of fruits and vegetables of different colours is a good guide.

Proteins contain the essential amino acids needed to keep us healthy. They are referred to as the building blocks of life and are found in every cell in the body. Include proteins in your diet by eating meat, fish, poultry, dairy products and soy-based products. Beans, lentils, nuts and cereals contain incomplete proteins, containing some but not all of the amino acids.

Starchy foods (potatoes, cereals, pasta, rice and bread) should make up one-third of your diet.

Choose wholegrain varieties and cook potatoes with skins on, if possible: they contain more fibre and fill you up for longer. Include at least one starchy food with main meals. It's a myth that starchy foods are fattening – gram for gram they contain fewer than half the calories of fat.

Sugar is considered the main culprit behind the wave of obesity in our society. Sugary foods also cause tooth decay. Monitor your consumption of sugary and carbonated drinks, cakes, biscuits, pastries and sweets, and cut down, if necessary. You don't need to be as concerned about the sugars found naturally in foods such as fruit and milk. Food labels can help: use them to check how much sugar foods contain. More than 22.5 g of sugar per 100 g means the food is high in sugar. Alcoholic drinks are high in sugar, as are some fruit-based drinks, such as smoothies.

Eat plenty of fruit and vegetables – at least five portions of different types a day. A glass of 100 per cent unsweetened fruit juice counts as one portion (but only one glass counts per day). Beware of fruit juice drinks, made from a mixture of fruit juices with added sugars.

Cut down on fat. There are two main types of fat: saturated and unsaturated. Too much of the former can increase the amount of cholesterol in the blood, which increases your risk of developing heart disease. Saturated fat is found in hard cheese, cakes, biscuits, pies, the fat on red meat, processed foods, cream and butter. Choose lean meat and cook with oil rather than butter. Eat foods that contain unsaturated fats, such as vegetable oils, oily fish and avocados.

Nothing need be off limits. However, foods such as hamburgers, pizza or pancakes shouldn't be eaten every day. You want to avoid eating these foods more than a couple of times a week at the very most. Consider things like chips or ice cream as an occasional treat, otherwise, there is a real risk of encountering weight problems.

cooking tips

- Measurements given in the recipes are for guidance only. Adjust seasonings and spices to your taste, add pasta to suit your appetite, or a couple of extra mushrooms rather than leave them to go to waste. Likewise, substitute ingredients you like for those you don't, and vegetables you have for those specified, providing the texture and density are similar.

- Ovens vary in temperature, so use the recommended temperature as a guide and reduce the heat a little if you find your oven runs too hot. Use your eyes and nose to decide when something is cooked and never be afraid to test that meat is cooked by removing it from the pan and dissecting, or sticking a knife in a broccoli spear to check it is tender.

- Follow the instructions. If the recipe says bring to the boil over a high heat, then simmer, do just that or you'll have dried up, undercooked or burnt food – burnt pans are hard to clean.

- Recipes in this book use sunflower oil, but vegetable or rapeseed oil are good substitutes. Olive oil is required where its flavour adds to the dish, but use the above alternatives if not available. Note: oils kept in the refrigerator may go cloudy, as the oils solidify slightly.

- The colour of a fresh chilli is no indication of its fieriness: it is the thin, small chillies that pack the punch. Removing seeds and membranes will reduce the impact of a fresh chilli.

- To skin tomatoes, make a score in the base of the tomato, cover with boiling water for 20 seconds, transfer to a bowl of cold water, then peel once cool enough to handle.

- 1 teaspoon dried herbs = 1 tablespoon chopped fresh herbs. Leftover fresh herbs can be chopped, put in ice cube trays and covered with a little water. Once frozen, store in a labelled zip-lock bag.

- Make salad dressings in a small screw-top jar.

- Use strong cheese in cooking. While Parmesan may seem expensive, you use a little of it; similarly use strong Cheddar cheese. You need to use a good deal more mild cheese to add flavour and you are getting a lot of added fat into the bargain. You can store commercially grated Parmesan in the freezer and use it from frozen.

food safety hints and tips

- Keep your kitchen and your hands clean.
- Store cooked and uncooked food separately to prevent cross-contamination and wash your hands and chopping boards between handling cooked and uncooked foods. Meat and fish should be stored on the bottom shelf in the fridge to avoid them dripping onto other foods.
- Always cool food before putting into the fridge.
- Freeze food as soon as possible after cooling, in sealed plastic containers or zip-lock bags, labelled and dated. Leave a gap in the bag or container for the liquid to expand as it freezes.
- Always defrost meat, seafood and poultry before cooking to avoid the risk of food poisoning. However, prawns are the exception to this rule.
- Store leftover canned food in Tupperware or bags, not the cans, and eat within a few days.
- Reheated food should be very hot to kill any bacteria. Never reheat food more than once. Note: cooked rice is potentially hazardous if not consumed within 24 hours.
- Cover food or wrap in clingfilm once opened to prevent drying out and contamination.
- Respect best-by dates and don't eat food that shows signs of mould or deterioration. Use your nose too – if it doesn't smell good, bin it.
- You are less likely to cut yourself with a sharp, effective knife.

the storecupboard

- salt
- black pepper
- sunflower or vegetable oil
- balsamic vinegar
- cider vinegar
- soy sauce (preferably reduced salt)
- tomato ketchup
- Dijon and wholegrain mustard
- mayonnaise
- tube or jar of garlic and/or ginger purée
- long-grain rice
- risotto (Arborio) rice
- dried pasta
- couscous
- stock cubes or powder
- canned tomatoes

- canned beans (e.g. cannellini, black, kidney, chickpeas)
- canned tuna and salmon
- canned or frozen sweetcorn
- frozen peas
- red lentils
- plain flour
- bicarbonate of soda
- baking powder
- cornflour
- dried herbs (mixed herbs, oregano, basil)
- spices (ground cinnamon, turmeric, chilli powder, paprika, red chilli flakes, medium curry powder, Thai curry paste)
- honey
- sugar (caster, brown sugar and icing sugar for baking)
- jars of antipasto, roasted red peppers, olives
- teas and coffee

perishable supplies
- butter
- eggs
- onions
- garlic
- vegetables and fruit
- meat, fish and chicken

basic equipment
- 2 or 3 sharp knives, including a serrated knife
- wooden spoons
- large spatula or fish slice
- potato masher
- garlic crusher
- pepper mill
- can opener
- vegetable peeler
- grater
- chopping board
- large mixing bowl
- sieve
- colander
- set of 2 or 3 saucepans
- non-stick frying pan
- baking tray
- medium roasting tin
- ovenproof and microwave-proof baking dish
- Hob-proof casserole or similar
- measuring scales
- small jug
- selection of airtight storage containers
- oven gloves
- tea towels
- assorted baking tins (as required)

using the microwave

Microwave cooking is great for students. So many people just use their microwave for heating up prepared food, but it's a versatile tool and many of the dishes in this book take advantage of the technology.

Microwave ovens transmit microwaves, which belong in the same category as radio signals, but at an ultra-high frequency. These waves bounce off the metal walls of the oven, penetrating the food and causing the liquid molecules to vibrate and heat up. Food will not heat in a metal container. Glass (not lead crystal), china and some plastics are microwave safe.

Different manufacturers offer ovens that function at different wattages. These recipes are tested on a 1,000 watt machine; if yours is more or less than this, adjust the timings accordingly.

The time taken to cook food in a microwave increases proportionately to any increase in quantity. As a rough guide, for double the quantity, add on half as much time again. So if one potato takes 5 minutes to cook, two will take 7–8 minutes.

Foods that have a fixed skin, like a potato, must be pierced before cooking to prevent steam building up inside and causing an explosion. An egg yolk is another example; it must be pierced a couple of times with a cocktail stick before microwave poaching.

Liquid foods must be stirred while cooking, as food on the outside of the dish cooks quicker than that in the centre of the dish.

Likewise, solid foods need turning. Be careful when stirring because some heated liquids can bubble without much warning. Similarly, many foods need to be covered to prevent splattering; a plate is good for this, or use clingfilm.

Food continues to cook for a few minutes after the oven has stopped and this is calculated into the cooking time.

a few basic recipes

Invest a little time in making a basic tomato sauce and a béchamel sauce for the freezer, so a great pasta, meat or fish dish, or a scrummy mac and cheese, is always available at the drop of a hat without resorting to cans or packets. And it's such a shame to throw out chicken bones; use them to make a stock for a soup on another day. Once prepared allow these dishes to cool, then package in individual portions in zip-lock bags, label, date and freeze.

basic tomato sauce
A classic recipe, used as a base for many stews, pasta sauces and soups.

For 4 Makes 600 ml (1 pint)	Bulk Makes 2.3 litres (4 pints)	Ingredients
2 tbsp	4 tbsp	olive oil
1 medium	2 large	onion, chopped
1 small	2 large	carrot, grated
2 or 2 tsp	8 or 2½ tbsp	medium garlic cloves, finely chopped
400 g (14 oz)	2 x 400 g (14 oz)	canned chopped tomatoes, drained
2 tbsp	125 ml (4 fl oz)	tomato purée
4 tbsp	225 ml (8 fl oz)	red wine or juice from the tomatoes
1 tsp	1½ tbsp	dried basil or oregano
		sea salt and black pepper

Heat the oil in a saucepan and add the onion and carrot. Cook gently over a low heat for 5–7 minutes until the onion is soft. Add the garlic and cook for 1 minute, then stir in the remaining ingredients. Season to taste. Cook for 10 minutes, or until the sauce has thickened. Leave the sauce chunky or purée with a hand-held blender.

basic béchamel sauce
The classic white sauce, this can be used as the basis of a creamy vegetable sauce. It's also good in a chicken or vegetable pie filling with ingredients such as spinach, mushrooms, ham or seafood. For a cheese-style sauce, stir in 125 g (4 oz) grated strong Cheddar cheese after the sauce has thickened.

For 4 Makes 350 ml (12 fl oz)	Bulk Makes 1.4 litres	Ingredients
2 tbsp	125 ml (4 fl oz)	butter or margarine
3 tbsp	175 ml (6 fl oz)	plain flour
350 ml (12 fl oz)	1.4 litres	milk
pinch	½ tsp	ground nutmeg
		sea salt and white pepper

Melt the butter or margarine in a saucepan, stir in the flour and cook over a low heat for 2 minutes, stirring constantly. Slowly add the milk, then increase the heat slightly and bring to the boil, stirring until the sauce thickens. Add the nutmeg and season. For a dairy-free version, use soy margarine or 2 tbsp sunflower or olive oil and soy milk in place of cow's milk. For a reduced-fat version, use 2 tbsp sunflower or olive oil and semi-skimmed milk.

chicken stock

Make chicken stock from a chicken carcass and fresh vegetables, vegetable scraps and peelings. Avoid using root ends, dirty scrapings and starchy vegetables, such as potatoes. Ensure a good mix of vegetables to avoid having a dominant flavour. This stock freezes well.

1 chicken carcass, including the skin
1 large onion, roughly chopped
1 carrot, scrubbed and roughly chopped
1 celery stick, roughly chopped
vegetable peelings (see note, above)
1 garlic clove, chopped
2 bay leaves
1 bunch of parsley
½ tsp salt
½ tsp whole peppercorns
water

Put the ingredients in a large pan and cover with water. Bring to the boil over a high heat, then simmer, uncovered, for at least 1 hour, preferably 2 or 3. Cool, skim off any visible fat, and strain. Use within 5 days or freeze. Makes approximately 2 pints.

For a vegetarian stock, omit the chicken bones and double the quantity of vegetables.

To save on freezer space, reduce the stock by half by boiling vigorously. Cool and pour into ice cube trays. When frozen put the cubes into a zip-lock bag. When needed, simply pop a frozen stock cube in a mug and add boiling water to dissolve the cube. Alternately, freeze in small plastic boxes.

breakfasts & brunches

The brain cannot function efficiently without fuel, so if you want to learn, don't skip breakfast. Of course, a bowl of cereal or a slice of toast will often be the quick and easy option at the start of the day, but on the weekend, or if you have an exam or a special presentation and you want to be at your best, spend a little time ensuring you give yourself a good boost in the morning. This chapter contains a few recipes for such occasions and also several speedier ideas for a healthy breakfast or brunch.

blueberry oat pancakes

see variations page 30

These pancakes are simple to prepare and, as they are made with yogurt, orange juice and oats, they are more nutritious and filling than most pancakes. Eat them on their own, with extra yogurt or with added sweetness in the form of honey or maple syrup.

1 egg
125 ml (4 fl oz) yogurt
125 ml (4 fl oz) orange juice
½ tsp vanilla extract (optional)
50 g (2 oz) wholemeal flour
2 tbsp caster sugar

1 tsp baking powder
¼ tsp bicarbonate of soda
40 g (1½ oz) porridge oats
pinch of salt
100 g (3½ oz) blueberries
½–1 tbsp sunflower oil

Break the egg into a bowl and, using a whisk or fork, beat in the yogurt, orange juice and vanilla extract, if using. Beat in the flour, sugar, baking powder, bicarbonate of soda, porridge oats and salt, until the mixture is smooth. Carefully stir in the blueberries.

Heat a medium-sized frying pan over a medium-high heat for a minute, then add just enough oil to lightly cover the base of the pan. Pour about 4 tbsp of the batter into the pan, then repeat, leaving enough space between each pancake to give them room to spread out slightly. Cook the pancakes for 2–3 minutes, or until small bubbles appear on the surface and the bases are golden, then use a spatula to carefully flip them over. When the pancakes are golden on both sides, transfer to a plate. Repeat with the remaining batter. Alternatively, keep any remaining batter, covered with clingfilm in the fridge, for 24 hours and stir well before using.

Makes about 10

chorizo beans on toast

see variations page 31

This classy, brunch-style beans on toast recipe is one of those breakfast dishes that is lovely at any time of the day. The recipe makes a delicious home-cooked beans dish but you could substitute a can of baked beans for a very quick alternative.

1 tbsp olive oil, plus extra for drizzling
1 chorizo sausage, thickly sliced
1 small onion, thinly sliced
1 garlic clove
400 g (14 oz) can cannellini or other beans, rinsed and drained

200 g (7 oz) canned tomatoes
6 tbsp chicken stock (made with ¼ stock cube)
¼ tsp mixed herbs
salt and pepper
4 thick slices of sourdough or wholemeal bread

Preheat the grill on a high setting.

Heat the oil in a pan over a medium-high heat, add the chorizo and cook, stirring occasionally, for about 2 minutes until lightly browned. Reduce the heat to medium, add the onion and cook, stirring occasionally, for about 5 minutes until soft and translucent. Meanwhile, cut the garlic clove in half lengthwise and finely chop one half, reserving the other half. Add the chopped garlic to the onion and cook for 1 minute. Add the beans, tomatoes, stock and mixed herbs, season to taste and simmer for about 5 minutes until the liquid is reduced by half.

Meanwhile, lightly grill the bread on one side. Rub the uncooked side of the bread with the cut-side of the reserved garlic. Drizzle the bread slices with a little olive oil and grill, turning once, until golden. Top with bean mixture and serve hot.

Serves 2

scrambled egg pitta

see variations page 32

This is a delicious way to eat your morning egg. The basic instructions given below for scrambled egg can easily be bulked up for more people and can be served on toast or alongside bacon and mushrooms.

1 egg
1 tbsp milk
salt and pepper
1 tsp butter

1 small tomato, chopped
chilli sauce (optional)
1 pitta bread

Beat the egg and milk with some salt and pepper in a bowl. Melt the butter in a frying pan set over a medium-high heat, then pour in the egg and cook over a moderate heat for 20 seconds. Stir with a wooden spoon, taking care to move the cooked egg from the base of the pan as it cooks. Remove the pan from the heat just before the egg is completely set – it will continue to cook after it is removed from the heat. Stir in the chopped tomato and a dash of chilli sauce, if using.

While cooking the egg, warm the pitta bread. Cut it in half and gently separate the top and bottom layers of bread to form a pocket. Fill with the scrambled egg.

Serves 1

french toast roll-ups

see variations page 33

These breakfast toasts are a special treat, yet are simple to make. You can prepare them the evening before you intend to eat them and leave them covered in the fridge, then all you have to do in the morning is cook them. The key to this recipe is to use soft white bread that rolls up easily and contains the filling without cracking.

1 large egg
2 tbsp milk
3 tbsp caster sugar
½ tsp ground cinnamon

8 slices of soft sandwich bread
8 tsp strawberry jam
2 strawberries or 8 slices of banana, chopped
1 tbsp butter

In a shallow dish, mix together the egg and milk with a fork, then set aside. In a separate dish combine the sugar and cinnamon, then set aside.

Cut the crusts off the bread, then flatten out each piece with a rolling pin to remove any air pockets. Spread a little strip of jam at one end of the bread and top with strawberry or banana. Roll up like a Swiss roll. Dip the roll-ups in the egg and milk mixture, turning carefully to ensure they are evenly coated.

Heat a frying pan over a medium heat for 1 minute. Add the butter and, once melted, add the roll-ups with the seam side facing down to seal. Cook until golden brown, then turn and continue to cook until golden all over. Remove the rolls from the pan one at a time and roll in the sugar-cinnamon mixture to coat. Serve immediately.

Makes 8

overnight oatmeal with banana

see variations page 34

Breakfast couldn't be simpler – just assemble the ingredients the night before and it's ready to eat in the morning. This raw oat recipe is served cold, which is super healthy because most of the nutrients are preserved. The fresh berries and nuts add to the goodness but they could be replaced by a little crunchy muesli for texture. For a dairy-free version, use soy yogurt and soy or almond milk. Check out page 34 for a hot version.

25 g (1 oz) porridge oats
90 ml (3 fl oz) Greek yogurt
90 ml (3 fl oz) milk
½ banana, mashed

to serve
1 tbsp Greek yogurt
maple syrup
few almonds and fresh berries (optional)

In a 325 g (12 oz) jar or a small bowl, mix together the oats, yogurt, milk and mashed banana. Cover and refrigerate overnight.

In the morning, top with the additional yogurt and drizzle with maple syrup. Sprinkle with the almonds and fresh berries, if desired.

Serves 1

toasted bagel with cream cheese & grapes

see variations page 35

This pretty variation on a bagel with cream cheese comes with the refreshing taste of juicy grapes. If you haven't got any grapes to hand, try it with slices of peach or a sweet, crunchy apple. It is very simple to put together, but if you prepare this dish for a friend it will still look as if you have made an effort!

1 plain, raisin, blueberry or mixed-seed bagel
3 tbsp cream cheese (preferably low fat)
pinch of ground cinnamon

10 black seedless grapes, halved
10 green seedless grapes, halved

Cut the bagel in half, then toast it on both sides, either in a wide-mouthed toaster or under the grill. Spread each half liberally with cream cheese. Top with a light dusting of cinnamon and then with the halved grapes. Serve in 2 halves while the bagel is still warm.

Serves 1

tomato & avocado omelette

see variations page 36

This is one of those standard recipes that is useful to have in your repertoire for a last-minute meal, day or night. The variations on the fillings are limitless. Using this recipe, you can easily turn a few scraps of cheese, meat or vegetables into a satisfying, economical and nutritious meal. For instance, try this one with a little crumbled blue cheese, goat's cheese or feta cheese, or with a few torn basil or rocket leaves.

2 eggs
1 tbsp water
salt and pepper

1 tbsp butter
1 medium tomato, chopped
½ avocado, peeled, stoned and sliced

Break the eggs into a small bowl and beat with a fork until smooth. Stir in the water and season generously with salt and pepper.

Melt the butter in a medium frying pan set over a medium-high heat, tilting to coat the bottom of the pan with melted butter. Pour in the beaten eggs and, using a spatula or the back of a fork, gently draw the mixture at the edge of the pan to the centre as it sets, and allow the liquid egg to flow into the spaces created. When almost set, add the chopped tomato and avocado to one half of the omelette and cook for 1 minute to heat through. Fold the omelette in half to cover the filling and serve immediately.

Serves 1

greek yogurt & berry breakfast

see variations page 37

This breakfast couldn't be easier to make or more refreshing to eat. It doubles as a quick dessert too, maybe using a berry-flavoured yogurt. You could even layer it in a glass with muesli for an elegant fruit parfait. Greek yogurt is thicker and creamier than natural yogurt and contains up to twice as much protein and about half the carbohydrates. On the downside, it contains roughly one-third less calcium. It is also higher in fat, so take advantage of reduced fat and fat-free varieties.

175 ml (6 fl oz) Greek yogurt
runny honey, to taste
6 strawberries, halved

4 tbsp blueberries
1 tbsp mixed seeds (such as sunflower, pumpkin, sesame and flax)

Put the yogurt in a cereal bowl or glass dish and drizzle with honey, to taste. Top with the strawberries and blueberries and sprinkle over the seeds.

Serves 1

variations

blueberry oat pancakes

see base recipe page 17

maple, banana & raisin pancakes
Omit the blueberries. Make the batter adding 1 small mashed banana and 2 tablespoons raisins with the orange juice. Serve with maple syrup.

maple & bacon pancakes
Omit the blueberries. Make the pancake batter, preferably with vanilla, and add 1 tablespoon maple syrup. Once the pancakes are cooked, cover with a clean tea towel and keep warm. Cook 4 slices of bacon in the same frying pan until crisp. Serve the bacon with the pancakes, accompanied by maple syrup.

baby food pancakes
Omit the blueberries. Make the pancake batter, adding 6 tablespoons apple sauce, mango or other fruit purée to the mixture with the orange juice. (There are a good selection of fruit purée flavours in the baby food section of the supermarket.)

chocolate chip pancakes
Make the pancake batter using the vanilla and replacing the blueberries with 60 g (2½ oz) chocolate chips.

variations

chorizo beans on toast

see base recipe page 18

bean & egg burrito

Make the bean mixture using black beans and add ½–1 teaspoon chilli powder with the garlic, to taste. While cooking, beat an egg in a small bowl, pour into a lightly oiled hot frying pan and cook on each side for 2–3 minutes until set and golden. Cut into strips. Substitute 4 flour tortillas for the toast. Divide the beans and egg between the tortillas. Turn in 2 of the sides, then roll up the tortilla to enclose the mixture.

curried beans with naan bread

Omit the chorizo and bread. Make the bean mixture, adding ½–1 teaspoon medium curry powder, to taste, with the garlic. Serve with warmed naan or other flat bread.

cheesy beans on toast

Make the bean mixture, adding 1 ball of mozzarella, chopped into small pieces, just before serving. This is delicious either with or without the chorizo.

penne with chorizo & beans

Make the bean mixture and omit the toast. Cook 225 g (8 oz) penne pasta in plenty of boiling water for 10–12 minutes until just cooked. Divide between 2 bowls and top with the bean and chorizo mixture.

variations

scrambled egg pitta

see base recipe page 21

scrambled egg & ham pitta
Follow the instructions for the basic recipe, adding 1 slice of ham, chopped into bite-sized pieces, with the tomato.

scrambled egg & cheese pitta
Follow the instructions for the basic recipe. Before filling the pitta bread, spread the inside generously with reduced-fat cream cheese or herbed cream cheese.

scrambled egg & lox
Follow the instructions for the basic recipe, replacing the tomato and chilli sauce with 2 tablespoons chopped smoked salmon and, if available, 1 teaspoon chopped chives.

scrambled egg & avocado pitta
Follow the instructions for the basic recipe. Finely slice the flesh of half a peeled and stoned ripe avocado. Place the avocado slices into the pitta pocket before adding the egg.

variations

french toast roll-ups

see base recipe page 22

nutella & banana french toast roll-ups
Prepare the basic recipe using Nutella or similar chocolate spread instead of strawberry jam, and top with a few thin slices of banana.

blueberry french toast roll-ups
Prepare the basic recipe using cream cheese instead of strawberry jam, and top with a row of fresh blueberries. You will need about 55 g (2 oz) cream cheese and 70 g (2½ oz) blueberries.

orange french toast roll-ups
Prepare the basic recipe adding the grated zest of ½ orange to the egg and milk mixture. Use fine cut or jelly marmalade instead of jam and omit the fresh fruit. Serve with segments of orange on the side.

french toast
Make up the egg and milk mixture as directed. Soak the slices of bread in the mixture (there will be sufficient for 3 or 4 slices, depending on the size of your loaf). Cook as per the main recipe until golden on both sides. Serve sprinkled with the sugar-cinnamon mixture and some fresh fruit.

variations

overnight oatmeal with banana

see base recipe page 24

hot overnight oatmeal with banana

Make the overnight oatmeal using 150 ml (¼ pint) milk. In the morning, cook in the microwave on HIGH for 1 minute, then stir and cook for a further 30–45 seconds. Serve as directed in the basic recipe, omitting the yogurt.

overnight oatmeal with banana & peanut butter

Make the overnight oatmeal as directed in the basic recipe, adding 1 tablespoon peanut butter to the mixture. Serve as directed.

overnight oatmeal with dried fruit & nuts

Make the overnight oatmeal as directed in the basic recipe, omitting the banana and using instead 2 tablespoons each dried cranberries, chopped walnuts and chopped dates. Serve with fresh berries or sliced peach.

overnight pinhead oatmeal with apple & raisins

Make the overnight oatmeal as directed in the basic recipe, using pinhead oatmeal, which will be crunchier than porridge oats. Substitute ½ an apple, grated, for the banana. Also stir in 1 tablespoon each raisins and walnuts and a generous pinch of ground cinnamon. Serve with fresh berries.

toasted bagel with cream cheese & grapes

see base recipe page 25

muffin with cream cheese & jam
Replace the bagel with a toasted muffin and omit the ground cinnamon and grapes. In a bowl, combine the cream cheese and 1–2 tablespoons strawberry jam. Spread this over the muffin. Top with a few slices of banana or slices of strawberry. This works with blueberry, raspberry or cherry jam.

bagel with cream cheese, tomato & avocado
Omit the ground cinnamon and grapes. Top the bagel with a medium tomato, sliced, and the finely sliced flesh of ½ peeled and stoned ripe avocado. Add a few torn basil leaves, if available. Drizzle with a little balsamic vinegar, Tabasco or other hot sauce, if liked.

bagel with cream cheese & jalapeño
Omit the ground cinnamon and grapes. Toast a plain or seeded bagel as directed. Combine the cream cheese with 2 tablespoons finely chopped green pepper, 1 sliced jalapeño and salt and pepper to taste. Add 1 tablespoon chopped coriander, if available. Spread over the bagel and top with slices of tomato.

bagel with cheese & bacon
Omit the ground cinnamon and grapes. Toast a plain or seeded bagel as directed and spread with cream cheese. While the bagel is toasting, grill or pan-fry 2 slices of bacon until crisp. Put the 2 halves of the bagel together with the bacon in the middle. Some people like to add up to 1 tablespoon jam or sweet Thai chilli sauce.

variations

tomato & avocado omelette

see base recipe page 27

mushroom omelette

Before cooking the omelette, heat 1 tablespoon butter in the frying pan. Add 6 sliced chestnut
or white mushrooms and fry over a medium-high heat, stirring occasionally, for 2–3 minutes
until tender. Tip out of the pan onto a warmed plate and keep warm. Add a little chopped fresh
parsley, if desired. Use the mushroom filling instead of the tomato-avocado filling.

cheese & jalapeño omelette

Prepare the omelette as directed, adding 2 tablespoons grated Cheddar cheese and 1 chopped
jalapeño with the tomato. Allow the cheese to just melt before folding the omelette in half.
Serve with the uncooked avocado slices on top of the finished omelette.

spinach, tomato & feta omelette

Prepare the omelette as directed, adding 3 tablespoons crumbled feta cheese and a small
handful of baby spinach leaves with the tomato; omit the avocado. Allow the cheese to just
melt and the spinach to wilt before folding the omelette in half.

skinny, fluffy tomato omelette

Put 1 egg yolk in a bowl with the water and mix with a fork to combine. In a separate bowl,
beat 2 egg whites until they form soft peaks (the consistency of lightly whipped cream).
Gently fold the egg yolk mixture into the egg whites with a spatula. Proceed as directed
in the basic recipe, using low-fat cooking spray instead of butter. Sprinkle salt and pepper
over the cooking omelette. Add the tomato but omit the avocado.

variations

greek yogurt and berry breakfast

see base recipe page 28

greek yogurt with muesli
Prepare the basic recipe, adding 4 tablespoons muesli to the bowl before adding the yogurt. The fruit is optional.

greek yogurt with peaches & pecans
Prepare the basic recipe, replacing the strawberries and blueberries with a sliced, stoned peach and 2 tablespoons chopped pecans.

greek yogurt smoothie
In a blender, or using a stick blender, blend together the yogurt, 1 tablespoon honey, 125 ml (4 fl oz) orange juice, the strawberries and the blueberries. Omit the seeds. Other additions could include ½ teaspoon vanilla extract, 2 slices of avocado, 1 tablespoon protein powder, a small handful of spinach or 1 tablespoon cocoa powder.

cottage cheese with honey & berries
Prepare the basic recipe, replacing the yogurt with cottage cheese or some cottage cheese with pineapple.

eating on the go

When you're out for the day, it's all too easy to end up in a fast food restaurant at lunchtime, or to nip into a shop for a snack loaded with sugar and other ingredients that won't do you any favours. But with just a little forethought and preparation, you can leave home with a healthy lunch or snack that might be just the thing to help you resist the temptation of the chip shop or burger bar. So it's good for the pocket as well as your health.

no-bake energy bars

see variations page 52

These little energy bars are simplicity itself to make and so much cheaper than buying similar bars in the shop. Note that they are calorific, so eat with discretion!

3 tbsp honey
2 tbsp peanut butter
65 g (2½ oz) pecans

65 g (2½ oz) almonds
2 tbsp mini chocolate chips

In a small bowl, melt the honey for 30 seconds in the microwave until just melted. Stir in the peanut butter. Leave to cool (to prevent melting the chocolate chips when you add them).

Line a small baking tin with baking paper.

Mix the remaining ingredients into the honey and peanut butter mixture thoroughly. Press the mixture firmly into the prepared tin. Refrigerate for at least 1 hour to set, then slice into 6 pieces. Store in the fridge. Wrap the bars tightly in clingfilm or kitchen foil to transport.

Makes 6

hummus, pepper & carrot wrap

see variations page 53

This healthy wrap makes a great midday filler and requires less time to make than it takes to queue up to pay for a sandwich during a busy lunchtime.

3 tbsp hummus
1 wrap
few drops of lemon juice
pinch of ground cumin (optional)

1 small carrot, grated
2.5-cm (1-in) strip of red pepper, sliced
small handful of rocket, lettuce of your choice
   or baby spinach leaves

Spread the hummus over the wrap. Sprinkle with a few drops of lemon juice and a pinch of cumin, if using. Scatter the carrot and pepper over the hummus with the rocket, lettuce or spinach leaves. Roll up the wrap tightly, then cut into 2–3 pieces. Wrap in clingfilm or kitchen foil to transport. If not using immediately, keep refrigerated until it's time to leave.

Serves 1

big beef sandwich

see variations page 54

This is like the deli sandwiches that get your taste buds tingling. It has plenty of meat and a lot of flavour. Using lean roast beef keeps this sandwich relatively low in fat, yet high in protein. Other meats – such as ham, salami and pastrami – are higher in fat and/ or sodium. This sandwich is made with two slices of bread, but is equally good when made with a baguette, panini or any other substantial bread roll.

2 thick slices of wholemeal, rye or sourdough
   bread
1 tsp butter or low-fat spread
1 tbsp wholegrain mustard, horseradish or
   mango chutney

2 slices (125–175 g/4–6 oz) lean roast beef
2 tbsp shaved Parmesan cheese or Cheddar
   cheese
1–2 sweet dill pickles, sliced
2 iceberg lettuce leaves

Spread 1 slice of bread with the butter or low-fat spread and set aside. Spread the other slice with the mustard (or use horseradish or mango chutney, if preferred). Top with half the roast beef, the cheese, the dill pickle and the lettuce, then finish with the remaining meat. Sandwich together with the second slice of bread.

Slice in half and wrap tightly in waxed paper, clingfilm or kitchen foil. Refrigerate until ready to set off in the morning.

Serves 1

frittata

see variations page 55

This is a fabulous portable snack made with eggs and leftover potatoes. No potatoes? No problem! You can use whatever vegetables you have in the fridge. Peppers, mushrooms, chopped tomatoes and courgettes would all work well. The frittata can be eaten hot, warm or at room temperature. Allow it to cool completely, then cut it and wrap it in waxed paper and slip it into a plastic bag for transporting, or alternatively, put the frittata in a plastic container.

1 tsp olive oil
1 tsp butter
1 medium cooked potato, sliced
3 eggs

55 g (2 oz) grated Cheddar cheese or crumbled
    feta cheese
2 spring onions, sliced
snipped chives, to garnish (optional)

Coat the base and sides of a small ovenproof frying pan with the olive oil and butter. Put the potato slices into the frying pan and cook over a medium heat until they are just golden brown, turning once.

Meanwhile, in a bowl, beat the eggs and stir in the cheese and spring onion. Pour the egg mixture over the potatoes, shaking the pan to allow it to seep between the potato slices. Cook over a low heat for 8–10 minutes. The frittata should be firm underneath and slightly loose on top. Using a wide spatula, peel back one side to lift it off the base of the pan, then gently flip the frittata and cook until the underside is set. If you don't want to risk turning it, you can put the frying pan under a preheated medium-hot grill for 2–3 minutes to set the top. Garnish with snipped chives, if using, to serve.

Serves 2

rustic chicken pasta salad

see variations page 56

This is a great meal to take on a picnic with friends or to have for a lunch on the go. It uses salad dressing rather than mayonnaise, as it is safer to eat if left unrefrigerated for a while. The ingredients given are guidelines – you can mix and match to suit your tastes and the contents of your cupboard. Pasta doubles in quantity when cooked, so if a small mugful of cooked pasta in the salad isn't enough for you, cook more.

60 g (2¼ oz) pasta bows or penne
2 tbsp Italian salad dressing
½ tbsp pesto (optional)
2 tbsp finely chopped red onions or 2 spring onions, finely chopped
2 tbsp chopped sun-dried tomatoes

2 tbsp canned sweetcorn
6 cherry tomatoes, halved
½ small courgette, diced
225 g (8 oz) boneless skinless chicken breasts, grilled, cut into 5 mm (¼ in) slices
shaved Parmesan cheese (optional)

Bring a pan of lightly salted water to the boil. Add the pasta and cook for 8–10 minutes until just cooked (al dente). Do not overcook. Drain and rinse in cold water, then leave to cool.

Mix together the cooled pasta, salad dressing and pesto, if using. Gently mix in the remaining ingredients, except the Parmesan cheese. Transfer to a plastic container and sprinkle over the cheese, if using – it may get mixed into the salad while transporting but this doesn't matter.

Serves 2

not quite one-thousand-year-old eggs

see variations page 57

This is a tasty variation of the hard-boiled egg, which is the veteran of many a packed lunch or picnic. For runny, soft-boiled eggs, follow the instructions but remove the egg from the water after 3 minutes and serve unpeeled.

2 eggs
4 tbsp soy sauce or tamari
4 tbsp water or black tea

2.5 cm (1 in) piece fresh ginger, sliced
2 tbsp granulated or caster sugar

Put the eggs in a pan and cover with water. Bring to the boil over a medium-high heat, then reduce the heat to low, cover and cook, just simmering, for 10 minutes. Drain, then run cold water over the eggs until cooled. To peel, crack the shell, then gently roll the egg on the work surface. Peel, then rinse under cold water to remove any stray pieces of shell.

In a small pan, combine the soy sauce, water, ginger and sugar and bring to a simmer over a medium heat, stirring constantly, until the sugar is dissolved. Remove the pan from the heat and add the eggs. Using a spoon, roll them around gently in the soy mixture for about 15 minutes until the eggs have an even brown colour, then leave to sit in the mixture for 1 hour, turning occasionally.

Remove the eggs from the pan and leave to cool, then wrap them in clingfilm to transport. These eggs can also be eaten warm, maybe with a noodle and vegetable stirfry.
Serves 1

minted falafel pitta pockets

see variations page 58

Shop-bought falafel make great sandwiches. Stuff them into pitta pockets with salad vegetables and you are in for a lunchtime treat. Ideally, use fresh mint to make the sauce but dried mint is acceptable, especially if you are not eating immediately, giving the dried mint time to rehydrate. Remember to drain any excess liquid from the salad ingredients to minimise the risk of soggy sandwich syndrome.

1 pitta bread
4-6 falafels, depending on size
1 medium tomato, sliced
2.5 cm (1 in) piece cucumber, sliced
lettuce leaves, sliced

mint-yogurt sauce
2 tbsp Greek yogurt
¼ tsp lemon juice
¼ tsp olive oil
1 tbsp fresh mint or ½ tsp dried mint
pinch of salt

In a small bowl combine all the ingredients for the mint-yogurt sauce. Set aside.

Cut the pitta in half and gently separate the top and bottom layers of bread to form a pocket. Fill with the falafels, tomato, cucumber and lettuce leaves. Drizzle over the sauce. The sauce can be put in a small, sealed container and taken separately, then drizzled over the sandwich just before you eat, if preferred.

Serves 1

mango bean quinoa salad

see variations page 59

Quinoa is a grain native to South America that has a delicious nutty flavour and crunchy texture. In addition, it is rich in complete protein, making it an ideal food to eat on the go. Quinoa quadruples in size when cooked, so you will have some to spare for another meal – it is tricky to cook less than this quantity. This salad is suitable for vegans.

225 ml (8 fl oz) water
85 g (3 oz) quinoa
200 g (7 oz) canned kidney or mixed beans
3 spring onions, sliced

2 celery sticks, sliced
½ mango, peeled, stoned and chopped
grated zest and juice of 1 lime
1 tbsp olive oil

Salt the water and bring it to the boil in a medium saucepan. Rinse the quinoa, then add it to the pan, stir and simmer for about 12 minutes, until tender and the germ ring inside the grain becomes visible. Drain, then cover with a clean tea towel and leave to sit for 5 minutes. Allow to cool.

Put the cooked quinoa (or as much as you will eat) into a bowl. Drain the kidney beans, then add them to the bowl with the spring onions, celery and mango. Stir in the lime zest and juice and the olive oil. Pack the mixture into a plastic container. It will keep for 24 hours in the fridge.

Serves 2

variations

no-bake energy bars

see base recipe page 39

sour cherry energy bars
Make the energy bars as directed using 6 tablespoons each pecans, almonds and sour cherries.

chocolate-drizzled energy bars
Make the energy bars as per the basic recipe. Break 25 g (1 oz) dark chocolate into pieces and put in a small bowl or mug. Melt in the microwave on low for about 1½ minutes – the exact time will depend on your microwave. It is best to do this in bursts of 20 seconds, stirring in between to avoid overheating. Drizzle the melted chocolate over the prepared energy bars before chilling.

granola cereal bars
Replace the nuts with 65 g (2½ oz) granola and proceed as directed in the basic recipe.

seedy energy bars
Make the energy bars as directed, adding 1 tablespoon mixed seeds to the mixture.

hummus, pepper & carrot wrap

see base recipe page 40

hummus, egg & carrot wrap
Hard-boil an egg and allow it to cool (see page 47). Peel and slice the egg, then lay the slices over the hummus. Proceed as directed.

guacamole wrap
Substitute guacamole for the hummus. Proceed as directed.

hummus, roasted pepper & olive wrap
Substitute half a roasted pepper from a jar, well drained, for the red pepper. Add 4 sliced black olives. Make the wrap as directed. Other favourite antipasto storecupboard ingredients, such as artichokes or canned asparagus, could replace the roasted peppers.

hummus & chicken tomato wrap
Lay thin slices of leftover chicken or a slice of deli chicken over the hummus. Replace the red pepper with 1 medium sliced tomato. Proceed as directed.

variations

big beef sandwich

see base recipe page 43

big turkey sandwich
Replace the beef with turkey and use Dijon mustard as the condiment. A slice of Swiss cheese works well instead of the Parmesan cheese.

big cheese and slaw sandwich
Replace the beef with slices of Cheddar, Gorgonzola, Edam or Emmental. Omit the Parmesan. Use 2 tablespoons coleslaw, draining off excess liquid, instead of pickles. (See page 146 for a recipe for quick coleslaw.) Omit the dill and mustard.

big fish sandwich
Replace the beef with a can of sardines in oil, thoroughly drained. Gently cut the sardines in half lengthwise with the blade of a knife to flatten slightly (you can eat the soft bones) before assembling the sandwich. Replace the pickles with 4 sliced sundried tomatoes. Omit the dill and mustard.

club sandwich
In a frying pan over a medium-high heat, fry 2 slices of bacon until crisp. Remove from the pan and drain on kitchen paper, then leave to cool. Cut each slice in half. Make the turkey sandwich above using mayonnaise instead of butter. Omit the cheese and add 2 large tomato slices and the bacon. Omit the dill and mustard.

variations

frittata

see base recipe page 44

spanish omelette with chorizo
Add 125 g (4 oz) sliced chorizo when frying the potatoes. The chorizo will produce quite a bit of fat, so dab with kitchen paper to remove a little of the excess before adding the egg – don't remove it all because it is very tasty. Proceed as directed.

roasted pepper frittata
Add 1 chopped roasted pepper from a jar to the frying pan once the potatoes are cooked. Add ¼ teaspoon paprika to the egg mixture. Proceed as directed.

sweet potato & spinach frittata
Use leftover sweet potatoes instead of regular potatoes. Once the potatoes are browned, add 125 g (4 oz) frozen spinach and cook until the spinach has wilted and the liquid has evaporated. Proceed as directed.

mexican frittata
Once the potatoes are browned, add ¼ teaspoon chilli powder and cook for 1 minute. Add 1 chopped medium tomato, ½ sliced fresh jalapeño pepper and 4 tablespoons frozen or canned sweetcorn. Proceed as directed. Mozzarella is a good cheese to choose for this variation.

variations

rustic chicken pasta salad

see base recipe page 46

rustic tuna pasta salad
Replace the chicken with 150 g (5 oz) canned tuna in water, drained and broken into chunks.

rustic mozzarella pasta salad
Replace the chicken with 1 ball of mozzarella cheese, torn into pieces.

tortellini pasta salad
Replace the pasta with 125–175 g (4–6 oz) packaged chilled tortellini. Choose a vegetarian tortellini if you are going to carry this salad around unrefrigerated.

creamy pasta salad
Replace the Italian dressing with ranch, Caesar or blue cheese dressing.

not quite one-thousand-year-old eggs

see base recipe page 47

hard-boiled eggs with celery salt

Follow the instructions for hard-boiled eggs but do not peel – the shell is nature's packaging. Pour 1 teaspoon celery salt in a little paper or kitchen foil and twist to secure. To eat, peel the egg and dip it in the salt. Omit the last 4 ingredients.

hard-boiled eggs with olive oil & paprika

Follow the instructions above, omitting the celery salt. Combine ½ tbsp olive oil, ¼ teaspoon paprika and a generous pinch of salt in a small, sealed plastic container. Use the oil mixture as a dip when eating the egg.

egg sandwich

Follow the instructions for hard-boiled eggs, omitting the other ingredients. Peel and roughly mash 2 hard-boiled eggs with a fork. Combine with 2 tablespoons finely chopped spring onions or dill pickle. Mix with just enough mayonnaise to bind. Spread over a large slice of bread, top with shredded iceberg lettuce or watercress and top with another slice of bread.

thousand-year-old egg noodle salad

Make a salad from 1 handful each of spinach and beansprouts plus 2 handfuls of cooked rice noodles. Toss in 4 sliced water chestnuts from a can and 2 sliced not-quite-1000-year-old eggs. For the dressing, combine 1½ tablespoons olive oil, 1 tablespoon soy sauce, 1 teaspoon each honey, vinegar and water, and ¼ teaspoon each of ginger purée and garlic purée.

variations

minted falafel pitta pockets

see base recipe page 49

minted chickpea pitta pockets
Replace the falafels with 4 tablespoons well-drained chickpeas.

minted feta pitta pockets
Replace the falafels with 4 tablespoons diced feta cheese, well drained. Supermarkets sell marinated feta with herbs, which is delicious and would work well in the pockets.

falafel & rocket pitta pockets
Replace the lettuce with rocket.

falafel take-out salad
Put all the salad ingredients and the falafels into a plastic container. (This also works well with the chickpea or feta variations.) Either dress with the yogurt-mint sauce or take this in a separate sealed container. You could take the pitta to eat on the side, if liked.

variations

mango bean quinoa salad

see base recipe page 50

mango smoked turkey quinoa salad
Add 175 g (6 oz) chopped smoked turkey to the salad.

peach & smoked ham quinoa salad
Add 175 g (6 oz) chopped smoked ham to the salad and replace the mango with a peeled, stoned and chopped peach. If you are using peach from a can, select peaches in natural juice and drain well.

mixed veg quinoa salad
While the quinoa is cooking, cook 225 g (8 oz) mixed frozen vegetables in boiling water. Drain and cool, then add to the quinoa instead of the beans, spring onion and celery.

curried mango bean quinoa salad
Follow the basic recipe, but mix ¾ teaspoon medium curry powder, ½ tablespoon mango chutney and a pinch of salt into the lemon (if you don't have mango chutney you can use 1 teaspoon honey or maple syrup). Replace the celery with 10 cm (4 in) piece cucumber, chopped.

10 minute meals

When time is short, ten minutes is sometimes all you can spare to make something to eat. Here are a few ideas for such occasions so you don't resort to fast food. Instead, why not fix a sandwich with the filling spread evenly all the way through (unlike many premade sandwiches)? Or try its heated Mexican cousin, a cheesy quesadilla, which can be prepared in a flash. Or you could cook a pasta or noodle dish in ten minutes with the right ingredients.

quesadilla with tomato, cheese & chilli sauce

see variations page 81

This dish makes a great emergency snack – the tasty little sandwiches take no time to prepare and cook. Serve them alone or accompanied by guacamole or a spicy dip. Use the remaining tortillas to make filled wraps or to eat with chilli. Reseal the package using sticky tape or transfer to a zip-lock bag and keep for a couple of days. Alternatively, freeze for use another time.

2 soft flour tortilla wraps
50 g (2 oz) grated Cheddar cheese

2 medium tomatoes, chopped
2 tsp Thai chilli sauce or other chilli sauce

Put 1 tortilla flat on your work surface. Sprinkle over the grated cheese and chopped tomato. Drizzle 1 tsp chilli sauce over the cheese and tomatoes. Top with the other tortilla to enclose the cheese and tomato and press down slightly.

Heat a large frying pan (one that is large enough to hold the tortilla) over a medium-high heat. Using a wide spatula, or working carefully by hand, transfer the tortilla to the hot pan and cook for about 2 minutes or until the tortilla turns crisp and golden. Turn and cook the second side. The cheese should now be melted and holding the quesadilla together. Transfer to a board or plate and cut in half, then cut each half into 2 or 3 triangles.

Serves 1–2

ham, pea & pesto linguine

see variations page 82

A packet of fresh pasta is just the thing to pick up on the way home when you're feeling hungry. It cooks in minutes, giving you just enough time to assemble a few ingredients to toss into the bowl for a tasty meal. You will probably cook one-quarter to one-third of a 450 g (1 lb) packet. Divide the remaining pasta into portions and put them in plastic bags, then seal and freeze them. When needed, cook them from frozen – it only takes about a minute longer.

125 g (4 oz) fresh linguine
3 tbsp frozen peas
50 g (2 oz) cooked ham or Parma-style ham
6 cherry tomatoes

2 tsp pesto
salt and pepper
grated Parmesan or Cheddar cheese,
   to serve

Bring a pan of water to the boil, add the linguine and peas and cook for 3–4 minutes until the pasta is just tender (al dente).

Meanwhile, tear or chop the ham into small pieces. Chop the cherry tomatoes in half.

Drain the pasta, stir in the pesto, then toss in the ham and cherry tomatoes, and season to taste with salt and pepper. Serve sprinkled with the grated cheese.

Serves 1

mozzarella & tomato salad

see variations page 83

This salad is often served as a starter in Italian restaurants under the name 'insalata caprese' – it was originally served on the island of Capri as a tastebud-tingling light lunch. It looks particularly pretty with multi-coloured tomatoes. You can serve it with some chunky bread or mix it into leftover pasta if you need something more sturdy. The recipe is easy to bulk up for friends.

175 g (6 oz) tomatoes (either 1 large or several small tomatoes)
125 g (4 oz) fresh mozzarella, cut into 5 mm (¼ in) thick slices

few fresh basil, parsley or rocket leaves
¼ tsp dried oregano
1 tbsp extra-virgin olive oil
salt and pepper

Prepare the tomatoes as appropriate (slice large or medium tomatoes; the small ones are best cut in half).

On a plate, arrange the tomatoes, mozzarella slices and basil, parsley or rocket leaves, alternating and overlapping them. Sprinkle the salad with oregano and drizzle with oil. Season with salt and pepper.

Serves 1

chicken not pot noodles

see variations page 84

This really is the ultimate quick meal – it will take you just a few minutes to prepare the vegetables, then pour over boiling water and leave this meal to 'cook' on its own. Make sure you choose noodles that will soften in boiling water without the need for cooking. Providing you have access to boiling water, you can prepare the ingredients in a preserving jar or jam jar and take them with you for lunch – leave out the lemon juice and just pop a lemon wedge into the jar to squeeze over at the last moment instead.

1 nest of quick-cook thin egg noodles or
   vermicelli
50 g (2 oz) shredded cooked chicken
¼ tsp chicken stock powder or ¼ crumbled
   stock cube
1 small carrot, coarsely grated
2 spring onions, trimmed and finely sliced
4 tbsp frozen or canned sweetcorn or peas

10 baby spinach leaves, finely sliced
½ tsp ginger purée (optional)
½ tsp garlic purée (optional)
generous pinch of black pepper
1 tsp soy sauce
squeeze of lemon juice

Put all the ingredients, except the lemon juice, in a heatproof covered bowl or jar. Pour over enough boiling water to just cover everything and press the ingredients down into the water with the back of a spoon.

Cover and leave for 8 minutes, stirring once. Stir in the lemon juice. Eat from the jar or transfer to a pasta bowl.

Serves 1

turkey & avocado sandwich

see variations page 85

A good sandwich has all the components of a good meal. This one has protein in the form of turkey and cream cheese, vitamins and minerals in the raw vegetables and fibre in the bread.

2 tbsp low-fat cream cheese
2 thick slices of wholemeal or rye bread
1 slice of roasted turkey
¼ avocado, thinly sliced

4 slices of tomato
2 iceberg lettuce leaves, shredded
1 tbsp cranberry sauce (optional)

Spread the cream cheese on one side of both slices of bread. Top one slice with turkey, avocado, tomato and lettuce.

Spread cranberry sauce on top of the cream cheese on the other slice of bread and sandwich the 2 halves together. Cut in half to serve.

Serves 1

spicy pepperoni french bread pizza

see variations page 86

This is one of those versatile meals that can be made from whatever you have to hand. Individual or small French baguettes are often reduced in price in the supermarket later on in the day, so grab a couple when you have the chance and stick them in the freezer. If you haven't got any French bread, panini makes a good substitute.

1 individual French baguette
2 tbsp tomato purée or tomato sauce
¼ tsp dried basil or oregano
pinch of red chilli flakes

5 tbsp grated Cheddar cheese
1 small tomato, sliced
12 thin slices of pepperoni
black pepper

Preheat the grill on a medium-high setting.

Cut the French bead in half and spread the tomato purée or sauce over the cut surfaces of the bread. Sprinkle with the dried basil or oregano and chilli flakes, then with the grated cheese. Top with slices of tomato and pepperoni. Season with black pepper.

Grill the pizzas for 2–4 minutes until the cheese begins to bubble and turn golden.

Makes 1 large or 2 small servings

lemon fish

see variations page 87

Fish is so quick and easy to cook and is wonderfully healthy, too. If you haven't cooked it before, this is a great recipe to start with. The recipe provides both grilling and microwaving instructions. If you use a thicker piece of fish, such as halibut, you will need to add a couple of minutes to the cooking time. The classic accompaniment to this dish is wilted spinach and some boiled new potatoes.

1 tbsp olive oil
2 white fish fillets such as cod, haddock,
    whiting or sole
salt and pepper

juice of ½ lemon
¼ tsp grated lemon zest
¼ tsp paprika
chopped parsley

Brush the grill pan or microwave-safe dish with oil. Place the fish fillets on the pan and season. Drizzle with the remaining oil and the lemon juice, and sprinkle over the grated zest.

To grill: preheat the grill on a high setting. Cook for about 5 minutes without turning but baste with the lemon juice 3 times. The fish is cooked when it turns opaque and flakes easily.

To microwave: when arranging the fish in the dish, put the thickest side facing the outside of the dish and tuck under any very thin bits. Cover and cook on HIGH for 3 minutes. If the fish is not opaque throughout, cook for another 1–2 minutes, checking every 20 seconds.

Sprinkle paprika and parsley over the cooked fish to serve.

Serves 2

power-up roughie

see variations page 88

A roughie is a smoothie made without a blender. If you have a blender, by all means use it to turn this into a smoothie. These drinks offer a great way to recharge the batteries in the middle of the working day, or to soothe the system if you have been overdoing things! Any squashable fruit can be substituted for the banana (see the variations on page 88 for ideas).

1 medium ripe banana, peeled
4 tbsp plain low-fat yogurt

about 225 ml (8 fl oz) orange and mango juice
runny honey

Slice the banana and put it in a bowl, then mash it to a really smooth paste with a fork. Add the yogurt and use the fork to thoroughly mix the banana and yogurt together. Transfer the mixture to a large glass. Pour in enough orange and mango juice to three-quarters fill the glass, then carefully stir the mixture with the fork until combined. Add honey to taste. Top up the glass with orange and mango juice, as necessary.

If you have a blender, blend all the ingredients together and pour into a glass.

Serves 1

bean & tomato pantry soup

see variations page 89

This soup is almost as quick to make as packet soup but it is much more wholesome and satisfying and doesn't have that synthetic flavour that you find with many commercial soups. You can enjoy this soup chunky or, if you have a stick blender, you can blend the soup until smooth.

1 tbsp olive oil
1 medium onion, chopped
1 small garlic clove, crushed
400 g (14 oz) can passata
400 g (14 oz) can cannellini or other
    white beans

125 ml (4 fl oz) water
1 tbsp soy sauce
1 tsp Worcestershire sauce
2 tsp mixed dried herbs, parsley, or oregano
salt and pepper
yogurt or grated cheese, to serve

Heat the olive oil in a medium-sized saucepan over a medium heat. Add the onion and garlic and cook for 4 minutes, stirring twice.

Put all the remaining ingredients, except the yogurt or grated cheese, into the saucepan. Blend with a stick blender, if you have one. Bring to the boil and simmer for 3 minutes. Serve in bowls topped with a spoonful of yogurt or some grated cheese, as liked.

Serves 2–3

stirfry prawns with noodles

see variations page 90

The stirfry has to be the best student meal ever – it's made in minutes and is both filling and healthy. Tossing in some egg or rice noodles gives you a full and balanced meal, from shopping bag to mouth in ten minutes. The recipe calls for a pak choi, which is just the right size for one. However, you could use half a packet of stirfry vegetables instead. Prepared vegetables tend to be more expensive but for a stirfry they provide a great variety of ready-sliced ingredients.

125 g (4 oz) thin egg or rice noodles
1 tbsp sunflower oil
½ mild red chilli, sliced
1 cm (½ in) fresh ginger, peeled and thinly sliced
1 small garlic clove, finely chopped

¼ red pepper, thinly sliced
2 spring onions, thinly sliced
1 small pak choi, thinly sliced
125 g (4 oz) small uncooked prawns, shelled and deveined
1-2 tbsp soy sauce

Bring a pan of water to the boil, then remove the pan from the heat and add the noodles. Leave them in the water to rehydrate or warm through, according to the packet directions.

Heat a wok over a high heat until very hot. Add the oil and swirl to coat. Add the chilli, ginger and garlic and stirfry for 30 seconds. Add the pepper and spring onion, stirfry for 30 seconds, then add the pak choi and prawns and stirfry for 2–3 minutes, until the prawns are cooked. Toss in about 1 tbsp water plus enough soy sauce to coat the veg and cook for 1 minute.

Drain the noodles, transfer to a large bowl or plate and top with the stirfry.

Serves 1

big mushroom sandwich

see variations page 91

Portabello mushrooms make a great vegetarian alternative to a meat burger. Select mushrooms roughly the same size as your bun (the really huge ones take longer to cook and will hang over the edge of the bun rather inelegantly). See the variations on page 91 for ideas for mushroom sandwiches made with smaller mushrooms.

2 portabello mushrooms
1½ tsp olive oil
few drops of balsamic vinegar
pinch of red chilli flakes
pinch of dried oregano or thyme

salt and pepper
1 garlic clove, cut in half lengthwise
1 ciabatta or crusty white roll, split
1 small tomato, sliced
lettuce or baby spinach leaves, cut into strips

Preheat the grill on a high setting.

Cut off the mushroom stems. Wipe the caps with damp kitchen paper. Combine 1 tsp olive oil and the vinegar and smooth the mixture over the mushrooms on all sides. Put the mushrooms, stem-side up, on kitchen foil or a small heatproof dish and sprinkle over the chilli flakes, herbs, salt and pepper. Place under the grill 7.5–10 cm (3–4 in) from the heat and cook for 6–8 minutes or until tender, turning halfway through the cooking time.

Meanwhile, rub the cut side of the garlic on the cut surfaces of the bun. Drizzle with the remaining oil. Put the bun under the grill with the mushrooms and toast until golden. Put the cooked mushrooms on the toasted bun and top with the tomato and lettuce or spinach. You can serve this as an open sandwich or place the two halves together.
Serves 1

chicken & black bean tacos

see variations page 92

This is one of those dishes that is always comforting to eat. It bulks up easily, too, so is a good one to make when someone calls by for a quick bite before a night out. The list of additions at the end of the ingredients is quite long – use any of them that you have to hand, in any combination.

sauce
175 ml (6 fl oz) passata
1 tsp vinegar
1/2–1 tsp chilli powder
1/2 tsp ground cumin
1 tsp dried oregano
pinch of sugar

1 tbsp sunflower oil
1 chicken breast, thinly sliced
salt and pepper
1/4 x 400 g (14 oz) can black beans, rinsed and drained
4 taco shells
4 tbsp grated Cheddar cheese
toppings: shredded lettuce, avocado wedges, sliced tomatoes, lime wedges, finely chopped onion, sliced cucumber, chopped coriander (all optional), to serve
4 tbsp sour cream or Greek yogurt, to serve (optional)

Mix all the sauce ingredients in a small bowl and set aside.

Heat a wok or frying pan over a high heat until very hot. Add the oil and swirl to coat. Season the chicken with salt and pepper. Stirfry for 3–4 minutes until cooked and white throughout. Pour in the sauce and beans and bring to the boil, then simmer for 3 minutes.

To serve, spoon the mixture into the taco shells and top with the cheese and any of the desired toppings, finishing with sour cream or yogurt, if liked.
Makes 4

cheese & tomato soufflé in a mug

see variations page 93

You will impress your friends with this cunning little recipe for a sophisticated soufflé. It is made in a large coffee mug and quickly cooked in the microwave (to cook in the oven, bake in an ovenproof dish for 15–20 minutes at 180°C/Gas Mark 4). To make two mugs, multiply all the ingredients by two and the cooking times by one and a half. You need to serve the soufflés as soon as they are cooked, as they sink on contact with cold air. This dish is perfect with a tomato-based salad and some fresh crusty bread.

1 tbsp and 1 tsp butter, at room temperature
1 tbsp grated Parmesan cheese or breadcrumbs
1 tbsp flour
pinch of salt
4 tbsp milk

1 large egg, separated
3 tbsp grated Cheddar cheese
¼ tsp ground paprika or nutmeg
3 baby tomatoes, quartered

Grease a mug with 1 tsp butter, then add the grated Parmesan or breadcrumbs and shake to coat the butter. Put the mug in the freezer while you prepare the soufflé mixture.

Melt 1 tbsp butter in a microwave bowl on HIGH for 30 seconds. Beat in the flour and salt. Stir in the milk and beat until smooth. Cook on HIGH for 20 seconds, beat and cook for a further 20 seconds. Add the egg yolk, cheese and paprika or nutmeg and microwave for 20 seconds. Beat until smooth. Stir in the tomatoes.

In a separate bowl, whisk the egg white until stiff. Fold half into the hot cheese sauce mix, then gently fold in the remaining half. Handle carefully to retain as much air as possible. Pour into the mug. Microwave on LOW for 1 minute, then on MEDIUM for 1 minute. Serve immediately. *Serves 1*

variations

quesadilla with tomato, cheese & chilli sauce

see base recipe page 61

quesadilla with beans
Replace the tomatoes with ¼ x 400 g (14 oz) can baked beans. Use the hot chilli sauce or replace with brown sauce.

courgette & blue cheese quesadilla
Use 25 g (1 oz) each of Cheddar and blue cheese. Replace the tomato with 1 small courgette, grated onto a sheet of kitchen paper and blotted to removed excess liquid. Omit the Thai chilli sauce.

quesadilla with peppers
Slice a jalapeño pepper and ¼ red or green pepper. Follow the basic recipe, sprinkling over the jalapeño and pepper slices.

quesadilla with tuna & cheese
Follow the basic recipe, adding 2 tablespoons drained, canned tuna over the cheese with the tomato.

ham, pea & pesto linguine

see base recipe page 62

prawn, pea & pesto linguine
Replace the ham with 50 g (2 oz) cooked peeled prawns.

goat's cheese, pea & pesto linguine
Replace the ham with 50 g (2 oz) chopped goat's cheese.

ham, pea & tapenade linguine
Replace the pesto with tapenade and a squeeze of lemon juice.

pea & lemon garlic linguine
Omit the ham, tomatoes and pesto. While the pasta is cooking, very finely slice ½ garlic clove. Once the pasta and peas are drained, return to the pan, pour over 1½ tablespoons olive oil and add the garlic. Cook, while tossing, for 1 minute. Add 1 tablespoon freshly squeezed lemon juice and cook for another minute. Season generously with salt and black pepper.

mozzarella & tomato salad

see base recipe page 65

mozzarella & tomato salad with balsamic vinegar
Drizzle about ½ teaspoon balsamic vinegar over the finished salad. This is
particularly good for adding flavour if you do not have any fresh herbs.

three-coloured salad
Cut ½ peeled and stoned avocado into thin slices. Add it to the salad, alternating
between the tomato and mozzarella slices.

mozzarella & salami
Alternate 6 thin slices of salami between the tomato and mozzarella slices.

corn caprese salad
Heat a small frying pan over a medium-high heat. Put 3 tablespoons frozen
sweetcorn directly in the pan – do not defrost. Cook until the corn is browned
all over. Leave to cool. Make the mozzarella and tomato salad as directed and
sprinkle over the corn.

variations

chicken not pot noodle soup

see base recipe page 66

thai curry prawn noodle soup
Replace the chicken with 50 g (2 oz) small cooked prawns. Add 1 teaspoon Thai curry paste with the other ingredients.

tofu noodle soup
Replace the chicken with 85 g (3 oz) chopped tofu.

miso beef noodle soup
Replace the chicken with 1 small, thin slice of raw beef, cut into strips. Use 1 packet of instant miso soup mix instead of the stock powder or cube. Add 1 small red chilli with the other ingredients.

peanut butter noodle soup
Add 1 tablespoon peanut butter and ¼ teaspoon each of white wine vinegar and runny honey with the other ingredients. Stir well, as it will take a while to incorporate. Sprinkle over 1 teaspoon sesame seeds to serve.

turkey & avocado sandwich

see base recipe page 67

warm salmon & avocado sandwich
Grill a 125 g (4 oz) piece of salmon fillet for about 3 minutes on each side until just cooked through. Allow to cool slightly, then use instead of the turkey breast. Eat while still warm.

turkey, avocado & coleslaw sandwich
Spread the bread with butter or low-fat spread instead of cream cheese. Pile 2 tablespoons coleslaw on top of the turkey and omit the cranberry sauce.

turkey & carrot apple sandwich
Combine 1 tablespoon each of grated carrot and apple. Stir in 1 teaspoon mayonnaise and ½ teaspoon lemon juice. Use instead of the tomato and cranberry sauce.

turkey salsa sandwich
Replace the cranberry sauce with 1 tablespoon chunky salsa.

variations

spicy pepperoni french bread pizza

see base recipe page 68

hawaiian french bread pizza
Make the French bread pizza, replacing the pepperoni with 2 slices of ham, torn into small pieces, and 1 pineapple ring from a can, well drained and sliced.

caramelised onion french bread pizza
Melt 1 tablespoon butter or oil in a frying pan over a medium heat. Add 1 sliced white onion and cook, stirring occasionally, until clear. Sprinkle over a pinch of sugar and continue to cook until golden brown. This will take about 15 minutes. Meanwhile, construct the French bread pizza as directed in the basic recipe, then replace the pepperoni with the caramelised onion.

french bread pesto pizza
Make the French bread pizza, replacing the tomato purée and herbs with 2 tablespoons pesto. For a vegetarian version, replace pepperoni with sliced peppers.

french bread leftovers pizza
Make the French bread pizza, replacing the pepperoni with leftovers from the fridge. A little cooked chicken, ham, tuna or sausage would be ideal combined with corn, broccoli, mushrooms, peppers, tomatoes or olives. Use up blue cheese, feta or goat's cheese, too. You need about 6 tablespoons of toppings per slice.

variations

lemon fish

see base recipe page 70

curried fish steaks
Replace the salt and pepper with about ½ teaspoon medium curry powder for each fish fillet. Use your hands to rub it into the top of the fish well. Cook and finish as directed, omitting the paprika.

parmesan-crusted fish
After drizzling the fish fillets with lemon juice and zest, sprinkle 1 tablespoon grated Parmesan cheese over the top of the fish. Do not baste. (Unsuitable for microwave cooking.)

baked lemon fish steaks
Preheat the oven to 200ºC (Gas Mark 6). Prepare the fish as directed and put in an ovenproof dish. Bake, uncovered, for about 8 minutes until opaque, basting halfway through the cooking time.

seared tuna or salmon
Prepare the tuna or salmon as per the base recipe, omitting the lemon juice. Heat a frying pan until very hot. Add the olive oil, heat for 20 seconds, then add the fish. Cook for 1 minute only on each side – the middle of the steak will still be pink. Serve with a drizzle of lemon juice, zest and the topping as directed.

variations

power-up roughie

see base recipe page 71

protein power-up roughie
Add 1 beaten egg to the drink. Be sure the egg is fresh. Do not eat uncooked eggs if you are pregnant or your immune system is compromised. As an alternative, add 1 tablespoon protein powder.

peach ice cream roughie
Make the roughie, replacing the banana with half a ripe, peeled and stoned peach and the yogurt with 1 scoop of soft vanilla ice cream.

chocolate banana roughie
Make the roughie with 1 banana, chocolate milk (or chocolate soy milk) and 1 scoop of soft vanilla ice cream.

strawberry orange roughie
Make the roughie, replacing the banana with 8 large strawberries and use orange juice instead of orange and mango juice.

bean & tomato pantry soup

see base recipe page 73

spicy black bean & tomato soup
Add 1–2 teaspoons chilli powder and ½ teaspoon ground cumin to the cooked onions and fry for 1 more minute. Replace the white beans with black beans. Squeeze the juice from ½ lime into the finished soup.

bean & smoked bacon soup
Chop 3 rashers of smoked bacon into small pieces and fry with the onion.

tomato & roasted pepper soup
Replace the beans with 325 g (12 oz) jar roasted peppers, well drained and chopped. Also add 1 teaspoon sweet or smoked paprika to the ingredients when cooking the soup.

coconut, bean & tomato soup
Make the soup using only 125 ml (4 fl oz) water. Add 125 ml (4 fl oz) unsweetened coconut milk to the finished soup. Omit the toppings.

variations

stirfry prawns with noodles

see base recipe page 74

stirfry prawns italian style
Omit the ginger and soy sauce. Add a pinch of dried basil or oregano with the pak choi.
When the prawns are cooked, add ½ teaspoon tomato purée and 3 tablespoons water.
Heat through and season to taste with salt and pepper.

chilli veg stirfry
Omit the prawns. Replace the soy sauce with Thai sweet chilli sauce and a squeeze of
lemon juice.

chicken stirfry
Replace the prawns with 1 small, thinly sliced chicken breast. Stirfry the chicken with the
chilli and garlic for 3–4 minutes until it is cooked and white throughout. Remove from
the pan and set aside. Proceed as directed, returning the chicken to the pan when
adding the soy sauce.

stirfried beef in oyster sauce
Replace the prawns with 1 thin slice of frying steak, cut into thin strips across the grain
(cutting it this way makes the meat tender). Stirfry the beef with the chilli and garlic for
about 2 minutes until it is browned. Remove from the pan and set aside. Proceed as
directed, returning the beef to the pan when the vegetables are cooked. Replace the
soy sauce with bottled oyster sauce.

variations

big mushroom sandwich

see base recipe page 77

creamy mushroom sandwich
Cut the portabello mushrooms into slices or use 125 g (4 oz) sliced chestnut or white mushrooms. Put the oil, vinegar and chilli flakes into a small pan with 1 teaspoon butter. Fry the mushrooms for 3–4 minutes, turning frequently until tender. Stir in 2 teaspoons sour cream or Greek yogurt. Serve on the toasted bun as directed.

mushroom wrap
Cook the portabello mushrooms as directed; cool and cut into slices. Lay the mushrooms in a row across the bottom of a tortilla. Spread about 2 teaspoons mayonnaise on top of the mushrooms and season with salt and pepper. Top with 4 mozzarella slices and a sliced roasted pepper from a jar. Roll each tortilla tightly, starting at the bottom and tucking in the filling as you roll. Cut in half to serve.

bacon & mushroom breakfast muffin
Prepare the mushroom sandwich as directed. While cooking the mushrooms, fry 2 rashers of bacon until crisp. Toast a muffin. Top with the mushrooms and bacon.

mushroom & cheese sandwich
Grill the mushrooms and toast the bun as directed. Put the mushrooms on the base of the roll and top with a slice of Cheddar or Swiss-style cheese or 2 tablespoons crumbled blue cheese. Return to the grill until just melted. Finish the bun as directed.

variations

chicken & black bean tacos

see base recipe page 78

cheese & bean tacos

Omit the chicken. Mix the sauce ingredients in a saucepan and add 175 g (6 oz) black or kidney beans and 6 tablespoons frozen or canned sweetcorn. Bring to the boil, reduce the heat and simmer for 3 minutes. Remove from the heat and add 50 g (2 oz) crumbed feta cheese. Proceed as directed.

minced beef & bean tacos

Omit making the sauce. Stirfry 225 g (8 oz) lean minced beef with the vinegar, chilli, cumin and oregano until evenly browned. Add the black beans and stirfry to heat through. Season with salt and pepper. Serve as directed.

prawn & bean tacos

Follow the basic recipe, replacing the chicken with 225 g (8 oz) peeled and deveined raw prawns. (If using cooked prawns, there is no need to sauté – just add them to the seasoned sauce and heat through.)

very quick ham & corn tacos

Omit the sauce. Combine 225 g (8 oz) chopped ham and 6 tablespoons canned sweetcorn to 150 ml (¼ pint) prepared mild or spicy salsa. You can heat it through or serve it cold. Proceed as directed.

cheese & tomato soufflé in a mug

see base recipe page 80

cheese & spinach soufflé in a mug
Replace the tomatoes with 10 baby spinach leaves.

sweetcorn & tomato soufflé in a mug
Replace the cheese with 3 tablespoons canned sweetcorn.

pesto cheese soufflé in a mug
Replace the paprika or nutmeg with 1 teaspoon pesto.

blue cheese & ham soufflé in a mug
Replace the Cheddar cheese with blue cheese and the tomato with
1 tablespoon finely chopped ham.

30 minutes to cook

Everyone needs a repertoire of fuss-free meals. Most of these recipes rely on only one burner on the stove, so are perfect for peak kitchen times when everyone wants to cook. Many of these recipes are simplified versions of more complex ones – they may not be entirely authentic but they are still very tasty. The magic pizza is a brilliant take on the original. Who would have thought you could make pizza from scratch in just 30 minutes?

spiced carrot & lentil soup

see variations page 109

This hearty vegetarian soup is delicious and satisfying on a cold winter's day. Serve with good-quality crusty bread and a lump of cheese for an inexpensive meal. Make sure that the pieces of vegetable are not too large or the soup will take longer to cook. If you have a stick blender, you could purée the finished soup.

200 g (7 oz) dried red lentils
1.2 litres (2 pints) vegetable stock
1 medium onion, evenly chopped
3 large carrots, washed (not peeled) and
    chopped or grated

1 garlic clove, finely chopped
1 tsp mild or medium curry powder
salt and pepper
Greek yogurt, to serve

Wash the lentils in a sieve under cold running water until the water runs clear.

Put the lentils and the other ingredients in a large saucepan. Bring to the boil, then simmer for 15–20 minutes until the lentils and carrots are soft. Adjust the seasoning to taste. Purée, if liked, and serve hot with a spoon of Greek yogurt.

Serves 3–4

sweet & sour pork

see variations page 110

The sticky takeaway version of this dish bears no resemblance to this mouth-watering meal, with its crisp, bright vegetables that are full of flavour and combine with the juicy tanginess of pineapple. It is traditionally served with noodles or rice but works well cross-culturally with couscous, polenta, or stuffed in a pitta, or even accompanied by some plain fresh bread.

225 g (8 oz) lean pork steak or tenderloin, trimmed of fat and cut into thin strips
1 tsp grated fresh ginger or ginger purée
½ tbsp soy sauce (preferably light)
1 tbsp sunflower oil
1 small onion, cut into 6 wedges
1 small carrot, peeled and thinly sliced on the diagonal
½ red pepper, sliced
10 cm (4 in) piece of cucumber, peeled, deseeded and roughly chopped

1 slice of canned pineapple in natural juice, drained and chopped (reserve the drained juice)

sauce
4 tbsp pineapple juice from the can
2 tbsp tomato ketchup
1 tbsp vinegar
½ tbsp soy sauce (preferably light)
½ tbsp granulated sugar
½ tbsp cornflour

Put the sliced pork, ginger and soy sauce in a small bowl and set aside for about 10 minutes while you prepare the sauce and chop the vegetables.

Put all the sauce ingredients in a separate bowl and mix well. Set aside.

Heat the oil in a wok or heavy frying pan over a high heat until hot. Add the pork and stirfry for 3–4 minutes until evenly sealed and the centre of the meat is no longer pink. Remove from

the pan and keep warm. Toss the onion and carrot into the same pan and stirfry for 2 minutes, then add the red pepper and stirfry for 2–3 minutes until the vegetables are tender but crisp.

Return the pork and any juices to the pan, give the sauce a quick stir, then add it to the pan. Bring to the boil, then immediately reduce the heat to a simmer. Add the cucumber and pineapple, then continue to simmer for 2 minutes or until the sauce has thickened.

Serves 2

vegetable cashew thai green curry

see variations page 111

This creamy vegetarian dish can be gently spicy or quite fierce, depending on your taste or mood. If it is your first time using a particular brand of Thai curry paste, add a little initially, then add more to taste, as they vary widely in strength! This dish goes well with a portion of sticky jasmine rice but is delicious with any type of rice or noodle. For non-vegetarian and microwave cheat versions, see the variations on page 111.

1 tbsp vegetable oil
1 small onion, sliced
125 g (4 oz) fresh baby corn
½–1 tbsp Thai green curry paste
400 ml (14 fl oz) can low-fat coconut milk
1 medium head of broccoli, broken into florets,
   stems sliced

4 chestnut or white mushrooms, sliced
⅓ red pepper, sliced
40 g (1½ oz) unsalted cashew nuts
1 tsp lime or lemon juice
pinch of salt
pinch of granulated sugar

Heat the oil in a wok or large frying pan, then add the onion and baby corn. Stirfry the mixture for 2–3 minutes. Stir in the curry paste and coconut milk, cover and simmer over a low heat for about 2 minutes. Add the broccoli to the pan and return to the boil. Cover and continue to simmer for a further 8 minutes, until the broccoli is almost tender.

Toss in the mushrooms and red pepper and return to the boil, then simmer for 2–3 minutes until the vegetables are tender but crisp. Stir in the cashew nuts and lime or lemon juice just before serving. Season with salt and sugar to taste.

Serves 2

penne with bacon & beans

see variations page 112

This is a reliable meal that always gets a thumbs up. Vary the quantities of the ingredients according to your appetite and the contents of your fridge. This is not fancy food but it will fill you up and satisfy you.

200 g (7 oz) dried penne or similar pasta
½ tsp oil
2 slices of bacon, chopped
½ small or medium red onion
1 garlic clove, finely chopped
½ x 400 g (14 oz) can chopped tomatoes

¼ x 400 g (14 oz) can beans (cannellini, black, pinto), drained
1 tsp dried basil, oregano or mixed herbs
salt and pepper
grated Parmesan or Cheddar cheese (optional)

Bring a medium pan of water to the boil and cook the penne for about 10 minutes or according to the package directions. When the pasta is just cooked through, drain it.

Meanwhile, heat the oil in a large frying pan and cook the bacon for 2 minutes until it just begins to release its fat. Stir the onion into the bacon and cook for 4 minutes, then add the garlic and cook for 1 minute. Add the canned tomatoes, beans and dried herbs. Bring to the boil, then reduce the heat and simmer for 5 minutes, stirring occasionally.

Toss the mixture into the drained pasta. Season to taste with salt and black pepper and serve with Parmesan or Cheddar cheese, if liked.

Serves 1

egg fried rice with prawns

see variations page 113

If you have frozen prawns and peas in the freezer, you've got this tasty dish as a storecupboard standby. I suggest you cook enough rice for four people, use some for this recipe and divide the remainder between three plastic bags and freeze as soon as it is cold. Brown rice is healthier but takes longer to cook, so is brilliant to have in the freezer. Remember – all rice needs cooling and freezing quickly otherwise it can cause food poisoning.

2 tsp vegetable or sunflower oil
1 garlic clove, sliced
½ red chilli, sliced
150 g (5 oz) cooked brown or white rice
4 tbsp frozen peas
1 egg, beaten

125 g (4 oz) medium cooked prawns, shelled
    and deveined
2 spring onions, sliced
2 tsp soy sauce
chopped coriander or parsley (optional)

Heat the oil in a wok or frying pan and add the garlic and chilli. Stirfry for 20 seconds. Add the rice and toss until very hot, then add the peas and egg and continue to toss until the egg is set. Add the prawns, spring onions and soy sauce, mix everything together, then stir through the chopped coriander or parsley, if using.

Serves 1

chicken fajitas

see variations page 114

A Tex-Mex classic. If you want it even spicier, add a few drops of chilli sauce. The ingredients can be prepared in advance, then covered and refrigerated in the marinade for up to 12 hours. This recipe serves two, but if you are on your own, eat one portion and make a wrap for lunch with the leftovers. Serve with tortillas (warmed in the microwave) and, for a feast, some good tomato salsa or guacamole and sour cream.

1 chicken breast, sliced
½ red onion, sliced
½ green pepper, sliced
½ red or yellow pepper, sliced
1 green chilli, sliced (optional)
squeeze of fresh lime juice

marinade
1 garlic clove, finely chopped
1 tsp ground coriander
1 tsp paprika (preferably smoked)
¼ tsp ground cumin
1 tsp dried oregano
1 tbsp olive oil
pinch of salt

Combine all the ingredients for the marinade in a large bowl. Add the sliced chicken, onion, peppers and chilli, if using, and toss to evenly coat everything in the marinade.

Heat a wok or large frying pan over a high heat until very hot. Tip in the contents of the bowl and cook over a high heat using a heatproof, wide spatula to keep the contents moving. Continue to stirfry for 7–8 minutes, until the chicken is just cooked through – if you overcook it, it will become dry. Cut open one of the thickest slices of chicken to check for doneness. The vegetables should be tender but crisp. Squeeze over the lime juice.

Serves 2

magic crust pizza margherita

see variations page 115

Keep some self-raising flour in your cupboard especially for this ingenious recipe, which offers a very simple way of cooking pizza. You can be as creative as you like with the toppings. The ideas on page 115 will get you started.

225 g (8 oz) Greek yogurt
150–175 g (5–6 oz) self-raising flour, plus more
    to dust
¼ tsp salt
1 tbsp pesto

3 tbsp tomato purée
salt and pepper
125 g (4 oz) torn mozzarella
1 medium tomato, sliced

Preheat the oven to 230°C (Gas Mark 8).

Put the yogurt, 150 g (5 oz) of the flour and the salt in a bowl and mix with a spoon until combined. Turn out the mixture onto a generously floured worktop and knead for about 5 minutes. Add a little extra flour to help the dough come together, as required. The dough is ready when it is no longer sticky and forms into a stretchy ball.

Using a floured rolling pin, roll and pull the dough into a rough circle about 5 mm (¼ in) thick. Don't worry if the shape isn't perfect! Spread the centre of the base with the pesto, then with tomato purée and season with salt and pepper. Distribute the cheese evenly across the surface and top with the tomato slices. Bake for 12–15 minutes until the crust has browned and the cheese has melted.

Makes 1

salmon and vegetable couscous parcels

see variations page 116

This is a cunning and simple way to cook a one-pot meal with almost no washing up. Make sure you seal the parcels well or the stock could pour out and scald you. Alternatively, use a cleaned aluminum takeaway dish and seal the top with foil instead.

oil or spray oil, to grease
150 g (5 oz) couscous
grated zest and juice of 1 lemon
1 small carrot, grated
1 small courgette, grated
1 tbsp chopped parsley or 1 tsp dried parsley

1 tbsp olive oil
salt and pepper
½ fish stock cube
boiling water
2 salmon fillets, 125–150 g (4–5 oz) each

Preheat the oven to 200ºC (Gas Mark 6). Cut 4 sheets of kitchen foil to 30 x 30 cm (12 x 12 in). Lay 2 sheets on a work surface and the other sheets on top to form double layers. Grease the centre of each square. Bring up the sides of each and tightly double-fold the top edge where the sides meet. Double-fold one open end to form a parcel. Crimp the edges to seal tightly.

Combine the couscous, lemon zest and juice, carrot, courgette, parsley and olive oil in a bowl. Season with salt and pepper. In a heatproof jug, crumble the ½ stock cube, then pour over 225 ml (8 fl oz) boiling water and stir to mix.

Divide the couscous mixture between the 2 parcels. Using your spoon, spread out the couscous slightly, then top with the fish.

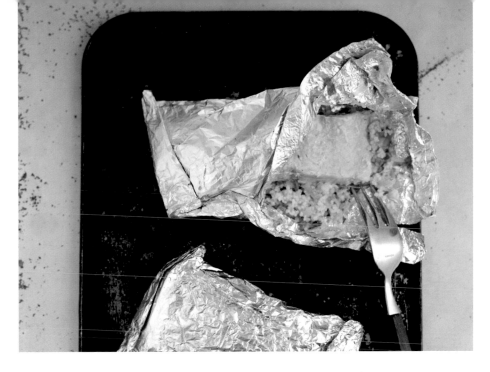

Put the parcels into an ovenproof dish (in case your seals are not tight) with the open ends facing the same direction. Tip the pan to raise up the open ends of each parcel slightly, then carefully pour 125 ml (4 fl oz) hot stock into each parcel. Fold over the openings very tightly, leaving room for the steam to circulate inside the packet as the food cooks.

Bake for 20 minutes. Remove from the oven and leave to rest for 2 minutes before making a small hole away from you to allow the steam escape, then open the parcel from the top. Eat from the parcel or transfer to a plate.

Serves 2

cheat's chicken satay

see variations page 117

Not one for the purists but this recipe makes a quick, simple and tasty meal. Serve it with rice or rice vermicelli and maybe some stirfried greens such as pak choi.

1 tbsp sunflower oil
2 spring onions, sliced
1 skinless, boneless chicken breast, cut into
    2.5 cm (1 in) pieces
1/4–1/2 tsp chilli powder
2 tsp soy sauce

1 tsp lime juice
1 1/2 tbsp crunchy peanut butter
1 tbsp unsweetened shredded coconut
    (optional)
1 tsp sweet chilli sauce or granulated sugar
4 tbsp water

Heat the oil in a frying pan over a medium-high heat and fry the spring onions for 2 minutes. Add the chicken and fry for 5–6 minutes or until cooked through and lightly browned. Pierce a piece to check that it is white throughout.

Add the chilli powder to the pan and fry for 1 minute. Add the soy sauce, lime juice, peanut butter, coconut, sweet chilli sauce or sugar, and water, then simmer for about 3 minutes, adding a little extra water if the mixture becomes too thick.

Serves 1

variations

spiced carrot & lentil soup

see base recipe page 95

spicy carrot, lentil & coconut soup
Add 400 g (14 oz) can coconut milk and reduce the stock to 575 ml (18 fl oz).

spicy lemon, courgette & lentil soup
Replace the carrots with 3 medium grated courgettes. Add the grated zest and juice
of 1 lemon.

curried parsnip & lentil soup
Replace the carrots with 3 medium parsnips, evenly chopped. Add 2 tablespoons mango
chutney or ½ grated apple with the other ingredients.

ham & lentil soup
Use only 1 carrot and add 125 g (4 oz) diced ham to the soup with the other ingredients.
Replace the curry powder with 1 teaspoon each of Dijon mustard and dried thyme or
mixed herbs. As the ham is salty, you shouldn't need to add salt.

bottom-of-the-fridge soup
Replace the carrots with about 225 g (8 oz) mixed vegetables – those you have left in
the fridge are ideal (such as beans, carrots, celery, parsnips, peas, potato, spinach, squash,
tomatoes or courgettes).

variations

sweet & sour pork

see base recipe page 96

sweet & sour chicken
Replace the pork with 1 large skinless, boneless chicken breast, thinly sliced.

sweet & sour tofu
Replace the pork with half a block of tofu cut into cubes and tossed in 1 tablespoon cornflour. Stirfry until evenly browned and crisped. Return to the pan when the sauce is thickened and serve immediately to retain crispiness.

pork & beansprout stirfry
Omit the sauce, cucumber and pineapple. Add 100 g (3½ oz) bean sprouts to the wok when the vegetables are just cooked and stirfry for 1 minute to heat through. While heating, add 1½ tablespoons soy sauce, 1 teaspoon rice vinegar (or ½ teaspoon balsamic vinegar), ½ teaspoon sugar and plenty of black pepper. Serve with a drizzle of sesame oil, if available.

very quick pork stirfry
Omit the sauce and vegetables. Stirfry the pork as directed. In the wok, stirfry 225 g (8 oz) frozen vegetables until just tender but crisp. Add 1½ tablespoons soy sauce, ½ tablespoon rice vinegar (or 1 teaspoon balsamic vinegar) and 1 teaspoon each peanut butter and sugar.

variations

vegetable cashew thai green curry

see base recipe page 99

thai red curry
Replace the Thai green curry paste with Thai red curry paste. Be aware that Thai red curry paste is made with red chillies and tends to be hotter than the green version.

prawn thai green curry
Omit the cashew nuts and add 225 g (8 oz) uncooked, peeled and deveined small prawns and ½ teaspoon fish sauce (optional) with the red pepper. The prawns should be opaque at the same time as the vegetables are cooked.

chicken & cashew thai green curry
Cut 1 skinless, boneless chicken breast into thin slices; add with the broccoli.

microwave vegetable thai curry
Put 225 g (8 oz) frozen mixed vegetables into a bowl and stir in ½–1 tablespoon Thai green or red curry paste and 225 ml (8 fl oz) coconut milk. Mix well and cover with a plate. Cook on HIGH for 4–6 minutes until the vegetables are just cooked. Add the cashews and a squeeze of lime juice. Leave for 1 minute, then serve.

variations

penne with bacon & beans

see base recipe page 100

beans & torn mozzarella on toast
Omit the pasta. Make the bacon and bean sauce and add about 50 g (2 oz) torn mozzarella to the finished sauce instead of Parmesan or Cheddar cheese. Serve on toasted sourdough or wholemeal bread.

penne with ham & beans
Omit the bacon. Sauté the onion in ½ tablespoon olive oil, then continue to make the sauce in the pan as directed, adding about 50 g (2 oz) chopped ham with the beans.

penne with tuna & sweetcorn
Omit the bacon and beans. Sauté the onion in ½ tablespoon olive oil, then continue to make the sauce in the pan as directed, adding ½ x 150 g (5 oz) can of tuna chunks, drained, and 4 tablespoons frozen or canned sweetcorn with the tomatoes.

penne with beans & sausage
Replace the bacon with 2 sausages. Sauté for about 12 minutes in 1 teaspoon vegetable oil to cook through and become crisp, turning occasionally; remove the sausages from the pan. At this point begin to cook the pasta and make the tomato sauce. Cut the sausages into slices and add to the sauce with the beans.

variations

egg fried rice with prawns

see base recipe page 101

egg fried rice with crispy bacon
Replace the prawns with 2 slices of bacon, cut into pieces. Stirfry for 3–4 minutes to crisp, then proceed with the basic recipe.

indian-style egg fried rice
Hard-boil 2 eggs and cut in half (see page 47). Omit the prawns. Proceed as directed, adding ½ teaspoon ginger purée and 1 teaspoon mild curry powder with the chilli. When the rice is hot, add the eggs and heat through. Stir in a few drops of vinegar with the soy sauce.

chicken & egg fried rice
Omit the prawns and follow the basic recipe. Add 85 g (3 oz) cooked chicken to the hot rice with the spring onions.

side of egg fried rice
Heat the oil and stirfry the rice until hot. Add half a beaten egg and continue to cook until the egg is set. Season with salt and pepper. Omit all the other ingredients.

variations

chicken fajitas

see base recipe page 102

beef fajitas
Replace the chicken with 175 g (6 oz) skirt or frying steak, cut across the grain into 1 cm (½ in) slices.

beany fajitas
Follow the basic recipe, omitting the chicken. After the vegetables have been cooking for 4 minutes, add ½ x 400 g (14 oz) can kidney or black beans, rinsed and drained, and 2 tomatoes, cut into quarters. Heat through and finish as directed.

lemon coriander chicken fajitas
Add the juice of 1 lemon, 1 tablespoon chopped coriander and ¼ teaspoon runny honey or sugar to the marinade. Proceed as directed. Omit the lime juice and sprinkle more fresh chopped coriander over the finished dish.

fish fajitas
Replace the chicken with 1 white fish fillet (such as pollock, cod or haddock). Brush the fish all over with the marinade, cut it into pieces and set aside. Proceed to cook the vegetables as directed. When cooked, transfer to a bowl and keep warm. Add 1 teaspoon oil to the pan and cook the fish for about 2–3 minutes on each side until just cooked through. Return the vegetables to the pan and cook for 1 minute.

variations

magic crust pizza margherita

see base recipe page 105

pepper pig pizza
Replace the tomato with 50 g (2 oz) sliced pepperoni and 30 g (1 oz) torn sliced ham.
Sprinkle over ½ teaspoon red chilli flakes.

chicken & mushroom pizza
Along with the tomato add 50 g (2 oz) shredded cooked chicken and 2 sliced chestnut
mushrooms.

antipasto pizza
Along with the tomato add 1 marinated artichoke, cut into quarters, 1 grilled red pepper,
sliced, 6 black olives, 10 mushroom slices and 1 sliced pickle. (Alter the ingredients according
to the contents of your jar of antipasto.)

spinach & egg pizza
Omit the pesto. Along with the tomato add 50 g (2 oz) frozen spinach. Distribute the
spinach, tomato and mozzarella around the pizza, leaving the centre free. Break an egg into
the centre and bake as directed.

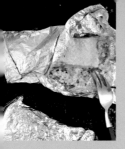

salmon & vegetable couscous parcels

see base recipe page 106

chicken & couscous parcels
Replace the fish with 6 small chicken tenders (mini fillets). Bake for 30 minutes.

moroccan fish parcels
Stir 1 teaspoon harissa paste and 2 tablespoons raisins into the couscous with the other ingredients.

mushroom & lemon couscous parcels
Replace the fish with 125 g (4 oz) mixed mushrooms (button, chestnut, oyster and portabello) cleaned, trimmed and cut into 1 cm (½ in) pieces. Add 1 finely chopped garlic clove to the couscous mixture.

creamy salmon parcels
Season the salmon generously with salt and pepper and put a piece of salmon in each parcel. Top with 1 tablespoon each of sour cream or crème fraîche, orange juice and chopped parsley. Put inside a foil parcel and bake as directed. Omit all the other ingredients.

variations

cheat's chicken satay

see base recipe page 108

chicken satay salad
Make the chicken satay, adding 4 tablespoons coconut milk to the sauce. Leave to cool. Make
a salad from shredded Chinese cabbage or lettuce and sliced carrot, cucumber, snow peas
and peppers. Pour the cooled chicken and sauce over the salad. Sprinkle over 1 teaspoon
toasted sesame seeds.

chicken satay wrap
Make the chicken satay. Leave to cool. There will be sufficient for 2 wraps. Lay 2 tortilla
wraps on a work surface and, in the centre, arrange some shredded iceberg lettuce and thinly
sliced cucumber. Top with the chicken satay. Fold the wrap to enclose all the ingredients and
cut in half.

spaghetti with chicken satay sauce
Make the chicken satay, adding 4 tablespoons coconut milk to the sauce. Cook 85 g (3 oz)
spaghetti in boiling water for 5 minutes, add 4 tablespoons frozen peas, then return to the
boil and cook for 3–5 minutes until the pasta is just cooked. Drain the pasta and toss with
the chicken satay sauce, then serve immediately.

quick, quick slow

These recipes can be started off quickly, then left to cook while you do other things. As all the effort is upfront, when you return to the kitchen, your meal is ready and waiting for you. Some recipes, like the stew and the tagine, give you quite a long cooking time to play with, while others, such as the cheese and corn bake, give you just enough time for a shower. Most are substantial and don't need much by way of accompaniment – a little rice or bread, maybe, or a green salad.

cheese & sweetcorn bake

see variations page 132

The lightness of this bake is balanced by its richness of flavour. You will find that this is a recipe you will return to again and again when there is little else in the cupboard, and you will always be pleased that you did. It works well with both white and wholemeal breadcrumbs, which you can grate directly from the loaf – it doesn't have to be super-fresh bread either! This bake is great served with a simple salad.

½ small onion, finely chopped
65 g (2½ oz) fresh breadcrumbs
50 g (2 oz) grated strong Cheddar cheese
75 g (3 oz) canned or frozen sweetcorn

1 egg, beaten
½ tsp Dijon mustard
225 ml (8 fl oz) milk
generous pinch of salt and pepper

Preheat the oven to 200°C (Gas Mark 6).

Grease a small shallow oven dish. Combine all the ingredients in a bowl and pour into the prepared dish. Bake for 40–45 minutes until set and golden brown on top.

Serves 2

just like mum's beef stew

see variations page 133

This is a good old-fashioned stew that has been made for generations. If you are in a hurry, you can omit the first stage of pre-browning the meat. This seals and caramelises the meat, adding flavour, but is not absolutely essential. Big stews improve with time, so it is fine to make this a day ahead and keep it refrigerated until required, or to freeze it in batches for a rainy day. You can leave out the potatoes and serve the stew with mashed potatoes, if you prefer.

900 g (2 lb) stewing steak, trimmed of visible
    fat and cut into 4 cm (1½ in) cubes
salt and pepper
2-3 tbsp olive or sunflower oil
2 tbsp balsamic vinegar
350 ml (12 fl oz) water
3 tbsp tomato purée
2 tbsp plain flour

1 large onion, cut into 2.5 cm (1 in) chunks
16 new potatoes, scrubbed
3 medium carrots, cut into 1 cm (½ in) rounds
350 ml (12 fl oz) beef stock
3 garlic cloves, finely chopped
2 bay leaves
1 tsp mixed dried herbs

Preheat the oven to 160°C (Gas Mark 3).

Pat the beef dry with kitchen paper, then season with salt and pepper.

In a large casserole or heavy ovenproof pot, heat 1 tbsp oil over a medium-high heat. Brown the meat in 2 or 3 batches, turning to brown evenly, cooking for about 5 minutes per batch and adding 1 tbsp oil for each batch. (If you attempt to sear the meat in 1 batch, it will not brown.) Transfer the meat to a plate and set aside.

Add the vinegar and about 125 ml (4 fl oz) water to the pan and scrape off all the crusty meaty bits that have stuck to the bottom of the pan (deglazing), as this will add flavour. Add the tomato purée and flour and stir until smooth. Return the meat to the pan with the rest of the water and all the other ingredients. Bring to the boil.

Cover, transfer to the oven and cook for 2–2½ hours until the meat is tender. Remove the bay leaves, taste and adjust the seasoning as required.

Serves 4 generously

keema curry

see variations page 134

Curry doesn't come any easier or less expensive than this! Adjust the amount of curry powder to taste, and you could add a chilli or two as well, if you like your curries hot and spicy. It is a good dish to cook in advance and heat up when you are hungry. Serve with naan bread and some chopped cucumber mixed with yogurt.

450 g (1 lb) lean minced beef or lamb
1 onion, finely chopped
1–1½ tbsp medium curry powder
3 medium potatoes, peeled and diced
175 ml (6 fl oz) beef stock

400 g (14 oz) can chopped tomatoes
salt and pepper
100 g (3½ oz) frozen peas
lime wedge and coriander sprigs, to serve
  (optional)

In a large frying pan, brown the mince and onion for 5–6 minutes over a medium heat (there is no need for oil, as the meat will release enough fat of its own). Use a wide spatula or wooden spoon to move the ingredients around in the pan, breaking up the meat into small grains and allowing it to brown evenly. Add the curry powder and potatoes and cook for 1 minute, stirring.

Pour in the stock and tomatoes and season with salt and pepper. Bring to the boil, reduce the heat, cover and simmer for 25–30 minutes or until the potatoes are cooked. Stir in the peas and cook for a further 5 minutes. Serve accompanied by a lime wedge and coriander sprigs, if liked.

Serves 3

no-fuss spag bol

see variations page 135

This is a core recipe for minced beef. Every family has its own special twist, so go ahead and add your favourite ingredient, although, truth be told, this basic version is delicious as it is. Do not buy over-expensive minced beef but avoid the cheapest, as it is high in fat. This recipe feeds four people, but you can freeze the sauce in individual portions if you do not need it all, and cook the spaghetti as required.

1 medium onion, chopped
450 g (1 lb) minced beef
2 garlic cloves, finely chopped
2 tbsp tomato purée
400 g (14 oz) can chopped tomatoes
1 tsp dried basil

1 tsp dried oregano
salt and pepper
350 g (12 oz) dried spaghetti
1 tbsp sunflower or olive oil
grated Parmesan cheese, to serve

In a large frying pan, brown the onion and mince for 5–6 minutes (there is no need for oil as the meat will release enough fat of its own). Use a wide spatula or wooden spoon to move the ingredients around the pan, breaking up the meat into small grains and allowing it to brown evenly. Remove from the heat and tip the pan to allow the fat to drain into one section of the pan. Remove the fat with a spoon and discard. You may need to brown the meat in 2 batches if your pan is small – overcrowding results in stewed, not browned, meat.

Return the pan to the heat and add the garlic, cook for 1 minute, then add the tomato purée, tomatoes, basil and oregano and season with salt and pepper. Reduce the heat and simmer for 30 minutes.

When you are ready to eat, bring a pan of water to the boil and add 1 tbsp oil. Add the spaghetti and allow the long strips of spaghetti to soften into the pan. Stir with a fork to separate the strands and ensure that all are submerged. Cook for about 8 minutes or until just tender. Drain in a colander and serve with the sauce and grated Parmesan.

Serves 4

panzanella salad

see variations page 136

This recipe is an inspired use of old bread, passed down from Italian peasants, for whom it was born out of necessity. It is best made with full-flavoured, slightly soft tomatoes. For the best visual effect, use different varieties and colours of tomatoes. If your bread isn't very dry, put it into a warm oven for ten minutes.

280 g (10 oz) ripe tomatoes, chopped
salt
150 g (5 oz) good stale bread (such as ciabatta,
    sourdough or French bread)
2 tbsp balsamic vinegar
1 small red onion, finely sliced
2 roast peppers from a jar, chopped

4 tbsp stoned black olives
1 tsp capers
1 garlic clove, finely chopped
3 tbsp olive oil
black pepper
10 sprigs of basil, torn

Put the tomatoes in a bowl, sprinkle with salt and put them in a colander to drain while you make the salad.

Tear the bread into pieces that are about the same size as the tomatoes and put them into a salad bowl, then moisten with the vinegar. Add the onion, peppers, olives, capers and garlic.

Squash the tomatoes slightly with the back of a spoon, then add them to the salad ingredients. Dress the salad with olive oil and plenty of black pepper, to taste. Toss to combine, then leave to sit at room temperature for 30–60 minutes. Sprinkle over the basil to serve.

Serves 2

meatloaf

see variations page 137

This is a versatile dish that can be served hot with gravy or tomato salsa (page 199), served cold for lunch, or even sliced in a sandwich. There are endless variations on this staple recipe but it is probably best when made with more than one type of meat. If you haven't got a suitable pan, then try the bacon-wrapped variation on page 137.

1 medium courgette, coarsely grated
675 g (1½ lb) minced beef, lamb and/or turkey
3 slices of bread, crumbled
1 egg
150 ml (¼ pint) milk
1 small onion, finely chopped
4 white or chestnut mushrooms, chopped

1 tbsp Worcestershire sauce
1 tsp oregano
1 garlic clove, finely chopped, or 1 tsp garlic purée
salt and pepper
4 tbsp tomato ketchup

Preheat the oven to 190°C (Gas Mark 5).

Put the grated courgette onto 2 sheets of kitchen paper and press out the excess water. Then put into a mixing bowl with all the other ingredients, except the tomato ketchup. Press the mixture into an ungreased 900 g (2 lb) loaf pan or ovenproof dish with a similar capacity. Spread the tomato ketchup on top.

Bake for 1–1¼ hours until firm, then turn out onto a serving plate and strain off any excess fat. Leave to stand for 5 minutes before serving with more ketchup or with a fresh tomato salsa.

Serves 4–6

sticky chicken drumsticks

see variations page 138

Chicken drumsticks are economical and, when cooked in honey and mustard, are easy to prepare. (This recipe could be made using chicken thighs, too. There are instructions on how to use ribs and sausages using the same formula in the variations given on page 138.) Serve with coleslaw or a herby tomato salad. Wrap the leftovers in foil and take them with you for lunch the next day.

4 chicken drumsticks
salt and pepper
2 tbsp wholegrain mustard

2 tbsp runny honey
1 tsp soy sauce

Preheat the oven to 175°C (Gas Mark 4).

Put the chicken drumsticks into a baking tray lined with baking paper. Sprinkle with salt and pepper.

Combine the honey, mustard and soy sauce in a bowl. Brush the mixture over the chicken.

Bake for 25–30 minutes, brushing the chicken with the juices once. Check that the chicken is cooked through by inserting a knife into the thickest part and easing open the flesh to ensure there is no pink showing and the juices are running clear.

Serves 2

spicy chorizo bake

see variations page 139

This dish is rich and delicious! Serve with a green side salad to balance out the spicy tomato flavour. To make it slightly less rich, you can omit the cream. You can prepare the pasta and sauce in advance, then cover and chill until required.

1 dried spicy chorizo, about 280 g (10 oz)
2 small red onions, chopped
2 garlic cloves, finely chopped
1 tsp red chilli flakes
2 bay leaves
400 g (14 oz) can chopped tomatoes, drained
125 ml (4 fl oz) water
¼ beef or chicken stock cube, crumbled

¼ nutmeg, freshly grated
1 tsp dried rosemary, thyme or mixed herbs
4 tbsp double cream
250 g (9 oz) pasta (use penne, rigatoni or orecchietti)
50 g (2 oz) crumbled goat's cheese or torn mozzarella cheese

Preheat the oven to 200°C (Gas Mark 6).

Remove the papery casing form the chorizo and crumble by hand or chop into small chunks of about 1 cm (½ in). This job is a bit messy.

In a large, dry frying pan, sauté the sausage meat, stirring until the meat is beginning to crisp and has released plenty of fat. Remove from the heat and tip the pan to allow the fat to drain into one section of the pan, then remove it with a spoon and discard.

Add the onion, garlic, chilli flakes and bay leaves to the pan and cook gently for about 5 minutes or until the onions are soft. Add the tomatoes, water, crumbled stock cube, nutmeg and dried herbs and bring to the boil. Remove from the heat and stir in the cream.

Meanwhile, cook the pasta in boiling water for 8–10 minutes until just cooked (it is important not to overcook pasta for baking). Drain the pasta and transfer to a shallow ovenproof dish. Pour over the sauce and mix. Sprinkle over the cheese. If cooking from hot, bake for 10–15 minutes, until bubbling; if cooking from cold, cook for about 30 minutes.

Serves 3

variations

cheese & sweetcorn bake

see base recipe page 119

spinach & cheese bake
Omit the sweetcorn and replace with 1 small handful of baby spinach leaves, roughly chopped, and add 1 teaspoon dried dill, if available. Any remaining spinach could form the basis of your side salad.

roasted pepper & cheese bake
Omit the sweetcorn and replace with 1 chopped roasted pepper from a jar. Add ½ teaspoon paprika and ½ teaspoon mixed herbs.

artichoke & pepper bake
Follow the recipe for the roasted pepper and cheese bake above, but add a roughly chopped marinated artichoke heart and a couple of chopped olives. This is useful for using up a jar of mixed antipasto.

corn & blue cheese bake
Follow the basic recipe, substituting crumbled strong blue cheese, such as Stilton, for the grated Cheddar.

variations

just like mum's beef stew

see base recipe page 120

beef & beetroot stew
Use only 1 large carrot. Add 2 medium beetroot, peeled and cut into 2.5 cm (1 in) chunks.
You may also substitute 150 ml (¼ pint) red wine for the water in this or any other of
the beef stew recipes.

beef & bean stew
Use only 8 potatoes and, 15 minutes before the end of the cooking time, add a 400 g
(14 oz) can of drained and rinsed cannellini beans.

beef stew with rice
Omit the potatoes and, 30 minutes before the end of the cooking time, add 75 g (3 oz)
long-grain rice, 50 g (2 oz) raisins, 4 tablespoons flaked almonds and 1 teaspoon sweet
or smoked paprika.

italian beef stew tomatoes
Add 200 g (7 oz) canned chopped tomatoes with the other ingredients.

variations

keema curry

see base recipe page 123

spinach keema curry
Replace the peas with 1 handful of baby spinach leaves and cook until wilted. Alternatively, add 50 g (2 oz) frozen spinach and cook for 3 minutes.

gingered keema curry
Add 1 teaspoon finely chopped fresh ginger (or use 1 teaspoon ginger purée) and 2 finely chopped garlic cloves with the curry powder. Squeeze lemon juice over the finished curry and garnish generously with chopped coriander.

cauliflower keema curry
Replace the potatoes with 225 g (8 oz) cauliflower, broken into medium-sized florets. Proceed as directed, cooking for about 20 minutes, until the cauliflower is tender. Finish as directed.

chicken & potato curry
Follow the basic recipe, using 450 g (1 lb) diced chicken instead of the minced meat. Gently cook the onions in 1 tablespoon oil for 5 minutes until soft and clear. Add the chicken and cook until white all over to seal. Proceed as for the basic recipe.

variations

no-fuss spag bol

see base recipe page 124

fancy spag bol
Chop 4 rashers of smoked bacon, add to the oil and cook until crisp. Add the onion, plus
1 celery stick, 1 carrot, ½ green pepper, all finely chopped, and cook for 5 minutes. Remove
from the pan. Brown the beef and add 4 tablespoons red wine, if liked, bubble for 2 minutes,
then add the bacon and vegetables and proceed as directed. Add 4 sliced mushrooms at the
end of the cooking time and cook for another 10 minutes.

sloppy Joes
Cook the sauce as directed. Using a spoon, pile the cooked sauce onto the base of toasted,
buttered crusty rolls and cover with bun tops.

greek lamb-stuffed peppers
Replace the minced beef with lamb. Cut 4 peppers in half lengthwise and remove the seeds
and membrane. Spoon the meat sauce into the pepper cavities and bake at 175ºC (Gas Mark
4) for 20 minutes. Sprinkle with crumbled feta cheese and bake for another 10 minutes.

vegetarian spag bol
Replace the beef with vegetarian mince, usually made from soy protein. It is fat-free and
cholesterol-free, so is good for weight-watching non-vegetarians too. Check the packet
directions for exact substitution instructions.

variations

panzanella salad

see base recipe page 126

panzanella with anchovies
Add 2 finely chopped anchovies from a can with the olives and capers.

greek bread salad
Add a 15 cm (6 in) piece of cucumber, unpeeled, deseeded and chopped, and 50 g (2 oz) feta, cut into cubes, to the salad.

spanish bread salad
Add 125–175 g (4–6 oz) dry chorizo sausage, casing removed and thinly sliced. If you choose uncooked chorizo sausages, sauté first, then cool before slicing.

goat's cheese & rocket bread salad
Replace the capers and olives with a handful of rocket leaves and 50 g (2 oz) crumbled goat's cheese.

variations

meatloaf

see base recipe page 127

meatloaf with cheesy spinach layer
Prepare the meatloaf as directed and press half the mixture into the pan. Sprinkle over 75 g (3 oz) grated Cheddar cheese and 50 g (2 oz) baby spinach leaves. Top with the remaining mixture and proceed as for the basic recipe.

turkey meatloaf with cumin
Use minced turkey only instead of mixed minced meat. Add 1½ teaspoons ground cumin and 2 tablespoons chopped fresh coriander to the mixture. Proceed as directed.

bacon-wrapped meatloaf
Shape the meat into a rectangular-shaped loaf and put it into a baking tray that has been lightly greased with olive oil. Spread ketchup on top of the loaf and arrange 7–10 bacon slices on top, tucking the edges underneath. Sprinkle with brown sugar and a pinch of cinnamon. Bake as directed.

quick microwaved meatloaf
Press the meatloaf mixture into a microwave-safe glass or plastic loaf pan, or a dish with a similar capacity. Spread with ketchup. Cook on HIGH for 15 minutes, then allow to stand and finish cooking for 10 minutes before serving.

variations

sticky chicken drumsticks

see base recipe page 129

sticky ribs

Replace the chicken with 450 g (1 lb) pork ribs. Cover the baking dish with kitchen foil. Decrease the oven temperature to 160ºC (Gas Mark 3) and cook for 90 minutes, turning and basting twice. Increase the temperature to 200ºC (Gas Mark 6) and cook for 10 minutes. As these take so long to cook, it's economically wise to double the quantities.

sticky sausages

Replace the chicken with 4 good, thick pork sausages. Thin sausages, such as chipolatas, will take a little less time to cook – about 20 minutes.

honey lemon drumsticks

Replace the mustard with the juice of ½ lemon and 1 finely chopped garlic clove.

chipotle satsuma drumsticks

Omit the sauce ingredients. Replace with the juice of 1 satsuma and 1–2 chopped chipotles in adobo sauce.

spicy chorizo bake

see base recipe page 130

sausage ragoût pasta bake

Replace the chorizo with 3–6 herby or other well-flavoured sausages, depending on size.
There's no need to remove the casings, simply cut them into 1 cm (½ in) slices and sauté
in 1 tablespoon oil, then proceed as directed.

meatball pasta bake

Replace the chorizo with 350 g (12 oz) prepared meatballs. Sauté in the frying pan in
1 tablespoon oil, then proceed as directed.

vegetarian sausage pasta bake

Replace the chorizo with 280 g (10 oz) vegetarian sausage. Heat 1 tablespoon oil and sauté
the sausages until lightly golden. Remove from the pan, then slice into 1 cm (½ in) pieces.
Return to the pan with the tomatoes. Proceed as directed.

eat-now chorizo ragoût

After adding the tomatoes and herbs, simmer the sauce for 10 minutes while cooking the
pasta. Stir in the cream and serve over the hot pasta. Omit the cheese.

bulk it up

It's great to be able to cook for a crowd. The recipes in this chapter mostly serve four but can be easily bulked up to serve eight, or even twelve. They are not difficult to cook and are suitable for a range of occasions. The tagine, ratatouille or risotto would be good for a supper party; the soup is great to come home to after watching a match; and the low-maintenance baked potato is perfect comfort food for a revision party. These recipes are also mindful of budget – none uses expensive ingredients.

pumpkin & prune tagine

see variations page 154

A great vegetarian all-in-one sharing meal. Don't be put off by the word 'prune' – after they have been slow-cooked they barely resemble their raw state and become soft, rich and incredibly sweet. If you are not convinced, use dried apricots, dates or pears instead.

1 tbsp sunflower oil
1 large onion, chopped
2 garlic cloves, finely chopped
1 tsp ground cinnamon
1 tsp ground cumin
1 tsp paprika
1 tsp turmeric (optional)
400 g (14 oz) can chickpeas, drained

400 g (14 oz) can chopped tomatoes
550 g (1¼ lb) pumpkin, cut into 5 cm (2 in) chunks
10 dried prunes, roughly chopped
475 ml (16 fl oz) vegetable stock
75 g (3 oz) bulgur wheat
2 tbsp yogurt, to serve (optional)

In a large pan, heat 1 tbsp oil over a medium-high heat until hot. Reduce the heat, add the onion and cook for about 5 minutes until soft. Add the garlic and cook for 1 minute. Add the cinnamon, cumin, paprika and turmeric and cook for 1 minute.

Tip in the chickpeas, tomatoes, pumpkin, prunes and stock. Bring to the boil, then simmer gently for 15 minutes. (If you don't need to eat immediately, prepare the recipe up to this point, then leave to cool, refrigerate and continue later.) Stir in the bulgur wheat, cover, then simmer for another 15 minutes until the vegetables are tender, the bulgur wheat is cooked and the liquid has been absorbed. Serve with a spoon of yogurt, if liked.

Serves 4

warming minestrone

see variations page 155

Minestrone is a guaranteed winner – everyone enjoys this wonderful, classic soup. To get the best of the vegetable flavours, sauté them in oil in the order given, which makes them truly luscious. The recipe suggests simmering the soup for 20 minutes, but some classic Italian cooks suggest 2 hours; the choice is yours!

2 tbsp extra virgin olive oil
1 large onion, chopped
3 garlic cloves, finely chopped
2 celery sticks, sliced
1 large carrot, chopped
175 g (6 oz) French beans, trimmed and cut
    into 1 cm (½ in) pieces
50 g (2 oz) cabbage, shredded
1 tsp dried basil

1 tsp dried oregano
salt and freshly ground black pepper
¼ x 400 g (14 oz) can chopped tomatoes
1.4 litres (2½ pints) vegetable or chicken stock
    or canned broth
400 g (14 oz) can kidney beans, rinsed and
    drained
75 g (3 oz) small pasta such as orzo
grated Parmesan cheese, to serve (optional)

Heat the oil in a large pan over a medium-high heat. Add the onion and cook for about 5 minutes until soft. Add the garlic and cook for 1 minute. Add the celery and carrot and cook for 2 minutes. Stir in the French beans and cook for 2 more minutes. Finally, add the cabbage with the basil and oregano, and salt and pepper to taste, then cook for 2 minutes.

Add the chopped tomatoes and the stock and bring to the boil. Reduce the heat and simmer for 20 minutes. Stir in the kidney beans and pasta and cook for about 10 minutes, until the pasta and vegetables are tender. Adjust the seasoning, if required. Serve in bowls with the Parmesan cheese, if using.

Serves 5–6

oven-baked risotto

see variations page 156

Risotto is cheap, tasty and filling. The only drawback is that you have to stand over the pot, stirring the rice, for the whole cooking time – but not with this oven-baked version. Serve this dish with roasted halved tomatoes and a green salad.

2 tbsp butter
1 small onion, chopped
300 g (10 oz) risotto (Arborio) rice
1.2 litres (2 pints) hot vegetable stock (made from a cube)

150 g (5 oz) frozen peas
125 g (4 oz) chopped ham
grated zest and juice of ½ lemon
salt and pepper

Preheat the oven to 200ºC (Gas Mark 6).

Melt the butter in a casserole or flameproof oven dish, add the onion and sauté over a medium heat for about 5 minutes until soft. Add the rice and then continue to cook for 1–2 minutes, stirring, until translucent. Pour over the hot stock, add the peas, stir, then bring to the boil. Cover with a tightly fitting lid and bake for 18–20 minutes until the rice is tender.

Stir through the ham and lemon zest and juice, and season to taste with salt and pepper. Cover and allow to rest for 3 minutes before serving.

Serves 4

chilli

see variations page 157

Every student should know how to cook this all-time favourite. It is one of the best recipes for bulking up and it tastes even better when reheated, making it the perfect choice to prepare in advance if friends are coming over to eat. Serve with rice or warmed tortillas, a bowl of guacamole or a green salad.

1 medium onion, chopped
450 g (1 lb) minced beef
2 garlic cloves, finely chopped
2–3 tsp chilli powder
1 tsp ground cumin
1 green pepper, sliced
2 tbsp tomato purée

400 g (14 oz) can chopped tomatoes
1–2 x 400 g (14 oz) cans kidney beans
75 g (3 oz) frozen or canned sweetcorn
1 tsp dried oregano
salt and pepper
sour cream, to serve (optional)

In a large frying pan, brown the onion and mince for 5–6 minutes (there is no need for oil). Use a wide spatula or wooden spoon to move the ingredients around in the pan, breaking up the meat into small grains and allowing it to brown evenly and release fat. Remove from the heat and tip the pan to allow the fat to drain into one section of the pan, then remove it with a spoon and discard. Note: you may need to brown the meat in 2 batches if your pan is not large; overcrowding results in stewed, rather than browned and sealed, meat.

Return the pan to the heat, add the garlic and cook for 1 minute. Add the chilli powder and ground cumin and cook for 1 minute. Add the green pepper and cook for 1 minute. Stir in the tomato purée, tomatoes, kidney beans, sweetcorn and oregano, and season with salt and pepper, then simmer for 30 minutes. Serve in bowls with sour cream, if liked.
Serves 4

baked potatoes with herbed cheese & slaw

see variations page 158

This is comfort food at its most homely and it offers an inexpensive way to feed friends. Unless you are lucky enough to have a food processor, cut the cabbage by hand using a very sharp knife and cutting as finely as you can. Grate the carrot. Local greengrocers or market stall holders will often cut you a half or even a quarter of white cabbage.

4 baking potatoes (russet or similar floury
    potato)
olive oil
salt
125 g (4 oz) cream cheese with herbs
snipped chives, to serve (optional)

coleslaw
2 tbsp mayonnaise
1 tbsp lemon juice
½ tsp Dijon mustard
¼ tsp granulated sugar
¼ tsp salt
¼ small white cabbage, finely shredded
1 large or 2 small carrots, grated
1 small onion, finely sliced

Preheat the oven to 200°C (Gas Mark 6).

To make the slaw, combine the first 5 ingredients in a serving bowl, then add the cabbage, carrot and onion and toss to evenly coat. Cover and set aside until required.

Scrub the potatoes under running water and pat them dry. You don't need to remove the eyes, but cut away any blemishes. Using a fork, prick 8–12 deep holes all over each potato,

so that moisture can escape while cooking. Using your hands, rub the potatoes all over with a little olive oil, then sprinkle with salt.

Bake the potatoes directly on the oven rack for 1 hour or until the skins feel crisp but the flesh below feels soft. (If you're cooking more than 4 potatoes, increase the cooking time by up to 15 minutes.) Serve by cutting a cross in the centre of each potato, then, holding it with a tea towel to protect from the heat, squeeze all 4 corners to squash the flesh out a little. Top each potato with a portion of cream cheese and serve with the slaw and snipped chives, if liked.

Serves 4

sausages with cheesy polenta

see variations page 159

Polenta is an excellent staple ingredient. Be sure to buy instant polenta or you will find yourself attached to the cooker for 50 minutes! Like pasta, instant polenta is dried and can be kept in the cupboard to use when there is little else to hand. It is simplicity itself to cook and, with a little cheese for flavouring, is delicious. Don't keep it just for sausages – it is great in all those situations that call for mashed potatoes.

8 good sausages (or sausage ring in portions)
225 ml (8 fl oz) milk
475 ml (16 fl oz) water
¼ tsp salt

175 g (6 oz) instant polenta
2 tbsp butter
50 g (2 oz) Cheddar cheese, grated
paprika, to garnish (optional)

Preheat the grill on a medium-high setting.

Line the grill pan with kitchen foil, if you like, to cut down on washing up. Grill the sausages for 10–12 minutes, turning occasionally, until cooked through. Make a small incision in 1 sausage to check that it is no longer pink inside.

Put the milk, water and salt in a small pan and bring to the boil. Slowly pour in the polenta in a thin stream, beating continuously. Stir for 3–4 minutes until it thickens and pulls away from the sides of the pan and the polenta is soft. Stir in the butter and cheese. Serve sprinkled with paprika.

Serves 4

ratatouille with pan-seared halloumi

see variations page 160

A ratatouille shouldn't be a dish of exhausted, overheated vegetables. It should retain a freshness that comes from cooking just enough for the flavours to fuse. Instead of halloumi, you could top with the lemon fish on page 70.

1 medium aubergine, chopped
salt
4 tbsp olive oil
1 medium onion, chopped
1 garlic clove, finely chopped
1 small red pepper, diced
1 small green pepper, diced

2 courgettes, sliced
400 g (14 oz) can chopped tomatoes
1 tsp dried oregano or mixed herbs
salt and pepper
250 g (9 oz) packet of halloumi cheese
juice of ½ lemon

Put the aubergine on a plate and sprinkle with salt. Leave to sit for 15 minutes to draw out the bitter liquid. Pat dry with kitchen paper.

Heat the olive oil in a large frying pan over a medium heat. Add the onion and cook, stirring occasionally, for about 5 minutes until soft and lightly golden. Add the prepared aubergine and garlic and continue to cook, stirring occasionally, for about 5 minutes until the aubergine is partially cooked. Add the peppers and courgettes and cook for an additional 5 minutes. Add the tomatoes, dried oregano or herbs and season with salt and pepper to taste. Bring to the boil, reduce the heat, then simmer for 5–10 minutes until the vegetables are tender.

Serves 3–4

Cut the cheese into 8 slices. About 5 minutes before the vegetables are cooked, heat a non-stick frying pan and sauté the halloumi slices for 2 minutes on each side – they should have just a little golden brownness to them. Serve the ratatouille with a little lemon juice squeezed over and topped with the halloumi slices.

real chilli burgers

see variations page 161

There is always the temptation to buy bargain-basement burgers for reasons of both time and economy. However, if you want to impress, make your own – they are simplicity itself to prepare and the reward exceeds the effort. Do not buy very lean minced beef, as the fat is essential to bind the burger together and keep it whole.

1 tbsp sunflower oil, plus extra for brushing
4 burger buns
1 large tomato, thinly sliced
shredded iceberg lettuce
mayonnaise
ketchup

burgers
450 g (1 lb) good-quality minced beef
1 small onion, very finely chopped
1 garlic clove, finely chopped
2 tsp ground cumin
2 tbsp tomato purée
2 tbsp sweet chilli sauce
1 tsp Dijon mustard
salt and pepper

Mix together the burger ingredients with your hands. Then, shape into 4 burgers, brush with a little oil and chill for 20 minutes.

Heat the oil in a large frying pan and sear the burgers over a medium-high heat until well browned on both sides. Reduce the heat and cook for 4–8 minutes on each side until cooked to your liking; keep warm.

Cut the burger buns in half and cook them, cut-sides down, in the hot pan so they soak up the delicious juices and become lightly toasted. Layer the buns with the burgers, tomato and lettuce, adding mayonnaise and ketchup, as liked.
Makes 4

variations

pumpkin & prune tagine

see base recipe page 141

lamb & prune tagine
Once the spices have been cooked, add 450 g (1 lb) lean cubed lamb, stir to coat in the spices and brown. Add the tomatoes, stock and prunes. Bring to the boil, cover and gently simmer for 1 hour. Tip in the chickpeas and 225 g (8 oz) pumpkin, diced, and cook for 15 minutes. Proceed with the bulgur wheat as directed.

chicken & prune tagine
Once the spices have been cooked, add 4 chicken thighs, stir to coat in the spices and brown. Add the tomatoes, stock and prunes. Bring to the boil, cover and gently simmer for 30 minutes. Tip in the chickpeas and 225 g (8 oz) pumpkin and cook for 15 minutes. Proceed with the bulgur wheat as directed.

sweet potato & prune tagine
Replace the pumpkin with 450 g (1 lb) peeled sweet potato, cut into 5 cm (2 in) chunks.

butternut squash & apricot tagine
Replace the pumpkin with 1 butternut squash, peeled, deseeded and cut into 5 cm (2 in) pieces. Replace the prunes with 10 dried apricots, cut in half.

variations

warming minestrone

see base recipe page 142

winter vegetable stew
Reduce the stock from 1.4 litres (2½ pints) to 700 ml (1¼ pints).

ham & pea minestrone
Omit the French beans and cabbage. Add 225 g (8 oz) lean diced ham with the tomatoes and 150 g (5 oz) frozen peas with the pasta.

tomato & basil soup
Replace the kidney beans with white beans and omit the cabbage and pasta. Replace the dried herbs with 2 tablespoons pesto. Add 4 tablespoons tomato purée with the chopped tomatoes.

mexican vegetable soup
Omit the basil. Add 1 teaspoon each chilli powder, ground cumin and ground cinnamon with the garlic. Garnish the finished soup generously with some chopped coriander and sour cream.

variations

oven-baked risotto

see base recipe page 144

mushroom & lemon risotto
Omit the peas and ham. Before cooking the onion, cook 225 g (8 oz) sliced mushrooms in 2 tablespoons butter. When soft, transfer to a plate, add the butter and onions as for the basic recipe and proceed as directed, adding the cooked mushrooms with the lemon.

cheese & tomato risotto
Replace the peas with 12 halved cherry tomatoes. Replace the ham with 125 g (4 oz) grated Cheddar cheese or 50 g (2 oz) grated Parmesan cheese. Omit the lemon.

spinach & pea risotto
When adding the peas and stock, stir in 125 g (4 oz) shredded fresh, or chopped frozen, spinach. Replace the lemon juice with 25 g (1 oz) grated Parmesan cheese. Omit the ham.

lemon prawn risotto
Add ½–1 teaspoon red chilli flakes with the stock. Replace the ham with 175 g (6 oz) small cooked prawns and heat through. (If using frozen prawns, stir them into the risotto after 15 minutes of cooking time to heat through.)

variations

chilli

see base recipe page 145

chorizo chilli
Follow the basic instructions, but use only 350 g (12 oz) minced beef and add 225 g (8 oz) skinned, crumbled chorizo.

vegetarian chilli
Follow the basic instructions, omitting the beef. When adding the green pepper, also add 2 chopped carrots, 2 chopped medium potatoes and half a medium butternut squash, chopped. Cook for 3 minutes, then proceed as directed.

chilli burritos
For each burrito, spoon chilli onto the centre of a tortilla; sprinkle with 2 tablespoons grated Cheddar cheese. Fold the top and bottom edges over the filling, then fold in the sides over the filling to enclose it. Repeat as required. Put the burritos, seam-side down, on a greased baking tray. Grill the burritos about 15 cm (6 in) from heat until crisp and golden brown.

tex-mex shepherd's pie
Boil 675 g (1½ lb) potatoes until tender. Mash with 4 tablespoons milk and 2 tablespoons butter, then season with salt and pepper. Put the chilli in a baking dish, top with the mashed potato and sprinkle with 4 tablespoons grated Cheddar cheese. Bake at 175ºC (Gas Mark 4) for 20–25 minutes until golden brown.

variations

baked potatoes with herbed cheese & slaw

see base recipe page 146

baked potato tuna melt

Scoop out the insides of the potatoes, keeping the skins intact. Mash the potato flesh with
4 tablespoons milk and 2 tablespoons butter. Add a 150 g (5 oz) can drained tuna,
2 chopped spring onions and 125 g (4 oz) grated Cheddar cheese to the potato mixture;
season and mix well. Pile back into the potato skins. Bake for another 15 minutes.

baked potatoes with baked beans & cheese

Omit the cream cheese. Heat a 400 g (14 oz) can baked beans and use 4 tablespoons grated
Cheddar cheese to sprinkle over the beans.

baked sweet potato with sour cream & slaw

Prepare sweet potatoes as instructed for potatoes, but put them on a baking tray lined with
kitchen foil. Bake for 50–60 minutes. Proceed as directed, substituting the herbed cream
cheese with sour cream mixed with 2 chopped spring onions.

microwaved baked potatoes

Wash the potatoes as directed. Cut a wedge out of each potato that is 3 mm (⅛ in) wide and
2.5 cm (1 in) deep (to prevent explosion). Put the potatoes on a microwave-safe plate and
cook on HIGH, uncovered, for 6 minutes, then turn over and cook for 4–8 minutes until a
fork goes through the centres. Leave to rest for 5 minutes. (If cooking 1 potato, cook for only
3 minutes, turn and cook for a further 2–3 minutes.)

variations

sausages with cheesy polenta

see base recipe page 149

pork chops with soft polenta
Cook the polenta as directed. Replace the sausages with 4 x 1 cm (½ in) thick pork steaks
or pork chops. Brush with oil and season with salt, pepper and a pinch of mixed herbs. Grill
for about 5 minutes on the first side, turn, baste with pan juices and repeat for the second
side. Check for doneness as for the sausages.

cheesy polenta with mushrooms
Cook the polenta as directed. Prepare the mushroom sauce as for creamy mushroom
sandwich (page 91) and serve with the polenta. Omit the sausages.

polenta slices
Cook the polenta as directed. Pour into a greased 20 x 25 cm (8 x 10 in) or similar-sized
dish and smooth the surface. Leave to cool, then chill in the refrigerator to set. Cut into
pieces and sauté these in a frying pan in 2 tablespoons oil or butter over a medium-high
heat, for 4 minutes on each side until golden.

spicy polenta
Cook the polenta as directed, adding 1 small red chilli, deseeded and finely chopped,
1 teaspoon mixed dried herbs, and ½ teaspoon garlic purée. Use as soft polenta or make
into slices following the instructions above.

variations

ratatouille with pan-seared halloumi

see base recipe page 150

ratatouille with kidney beans
Add a 400 g (14 oz) can kidney beans, rinsed and drained, with the tomatoes.

ratatouille wraps
Use leftover ratatouille to make wraps. Spoon ratatouille down the centre of a tortilla and wrap up over the filling. For a fancier version, spread the tortilla with tapenade (olive paste) before filling.

curried aubergine and peppers
After cooking the onions, add 1–2 tablespoons medium curry powder, to taste, and 1 teaspoon ginger purée and cook for 1 minute, stirring. Proceed as directed. Squeeze ¼ lemon into the finished dish. Indian paneer cheese could be used as a substitute for the halloumi.

ratatouille bake
Once the tomatoes and herbs are added to the vegetables, transfer to an ovenproof dish and add 2 small mugs full of cooked pasta (about 125 g/4 oz dry pasta). Top with 40 g (1½ oz) fresh breadcrumbs mixed with 4 tablespoons grated Cheddar cheese. Bake at 175°C (Gas mark 4) for 20 minutes until the top is golden. Omit the halloumi.

variations

real chilli burgers

see base recipe page 153

real classic burger
Make the sweet chilli burger omitting the cumin, tomato purée, sweet chilli sauce and mustard. Add ¼ teaspoon Worcestershire sauce instead.

blue cheese burger
Prepare the meat for the real classic burger above, but shape into 8 thin, 10 cm (4 in) wide patties. Mound 1½ tablespoons crumbled blue cheese (or other preferred cheese) on each of 4 patties, leaving a border. Cover each with one of the remaining patties. Press the edges tightly together to enclose. Cook as directed.

real meatballs
Prepare the meat as directed either for the sweet chilli burger or the real classic burger, above. Add 1 small beaten egg and 25 g (1 oz) fresh breadcrumbs. Mix well. Using wet hands, shape into 4 cm (1½ in) balls. Cook in a frying pan as directed, turning frequently; they will take about 10 minutes. Cook in batches, if required.

vegan burger
Mix 100 g (3½ oz) dry TVP (textured vegetable protein) with 175 ml (6 fl oz) boiling water and leave to stand for 10 minutes. Finely chop 1 small onion, 1 small carrot, 1 celery stick and 1 garlic clove; sweat in 1 tablespoon oil in a frying pan until just soft. Leave to cool, then add to the TVP. Flavour and proceed as directed. Use vegan mayo.

cooking to impress

With this collection of fail-safe recipes, you'll soon find you have a reputation for being a great cook. There are a couple of starters and a selection of main courses – some are economical and a few require you to push the boat out a little. Spaghetti carbonara is always popular and couldn't be easier to prepare as it requires almost no cooking, while the roast vegetable tart is a showstopper and will delight vegetarians and meat eaters alike. For fish lovers, you could serve prawn and coconut chowder followed by the excellent fishcakes.

prawn & coconut chowder

see variations page 178

This is an impressive soup that is cooked in under ten minutes. Thai curry paste varies hugely by brand, so be sure to add a little to start with and build up the flavour to taste.

400 g (14 oz) can unsweetened coconut milk
225 ml (8 fl oz) fish stock
1 jalapeño pepper, deseeded and thinly sliced
½–1 tbsp Thai green curry paste
¼ tsp granulated sugar
4 tbsp water

225 g (8 oz) shelled and deveined medium
 raw prawns
2 spring onions, thinly sliced
4 tbsp chopped basil
4 tbsp chopped coriander
1 lime, cut into wedges

In a large pan, combine the coconut milk with the fish stock, sliced jalapeño, curry paste, sugar and water and bring to the boil. Simmer for 3 minutes. Add the prawns and spring onions and cook for about 2 minutes until the prawns are just white throughout. Stir the basil and coriander into the soup and serve with lime wedges.

Serves 2–3

bruschetta with pesto & sundried tomatoes

see variations page 179

This reipe is simplicity itself and there is nothing wrong with that. Everyone loves these tasty morsels as a starter and they make an excellent canapé to serve with drinks on any occasion. They are inexpensive and easy to make in bulk, too.

8 slices of French bread or ciabatta
1 garlic clove, halved
8 tsp olive oil
190 g (6½ oz) jar of pesto

140 g (5 oz) jar of sundried tomatoes in oil,
    halved if large
basil leaves

Preheat the grill on a high setting.

Rub 1 side of each slice of bread with the cut side of the garlic clove to flavour the bread. Drizzle the outside edge of each slice with 1 tsp olive oil. Put the bread under the grill and toast lightly on each side.

Spread the pesto over each of the slices of toasted bread and top with sundried tomatoes and basil leaves.

Serves 4

carnivore's sharing board

see variations page 180

Sharing boards are popular in many restaurants and provide a sociable, informal start to a meal or a casual evening in with friends. The deli counter is laden with goodies, so take the ones suggested here as a starting point. Look for foods with a range of colours and textures and take a few minutes to fold salami in half or arrange the ham in rolls to look good. Choose an attractive loaf of bread to serve on the side.

8–12 oz selected cold cuts, such as Parma
    ham, salami, mortadella, roast beef,
    smoked chicken and smoked sausage
1 tbsp grainy mustard
150 g (5 oz) coleslaw (page 146)
150 g (5 oz) olives
8 cherry tomatoes
8 slices of ciabatta, French bread or
    sourdough bread

dipping oil
4 tbsp good-quality olive oil
1 tbsp balsamic vinegar
½ garlic clove, finely chopped or
    ½ tsp garlic purée
½ tsp dried basil or oregano
salt and pepper

Arrange the meats and the spoonful of mustard attractively on a chopping board or serving plate along with the coleslaw and olives in bowls. Garnish with the tomatoes.

Combine all the ingredients for the dipping sauce in a bowl and place this on the board or plate with the meat and the bread.

Serves 4

pork medallions
with lemon & parsley

see variations page 181

The thin slices of pork tenderloin cook through in the time it takes to brown them, so this is a very quick and easy recipe, which belies the sophistication of the finished meal. You can't get away with dried parsley for this recipe so you will need to buy fresh. Serve with some buttered new potatoes and some steamed French beans.

225–280 g (8–10 oz) pork tenderloin
salt and pepper
2 tbsp olive oil
125 ml (4 fl oz) white wine

juice of ½ lemon
1 tbsp chopped parsley
2 lemon wedges, to serve (optional)

To make it easier to handle, freeze the tenderloin for 20 minutes. Cut it into 8 mm (3/8 in) slices. Put these between 2 sheets of clingfilm and beat gently with a rolling pin or a frying pan until about half their original thickness. Season with a little salt and pepper.

Heat half the oil in a large frying pan over a medium heat. Add sufficient pork pieces to fill the frying pan without overcrowding, then sauté for about 2–3 minutes on each side until evenly browned. Remove from the pan, keep warm and repeat with another batch, adding more oil, as necessary. Once browned, add the wine to the empty pan, cook until reduced by about half, then add the lemon juice and parsley. Arrange the meat on warmed plates and spoon over the sauce (there isn't a great deal but it is delicious). Serve with lemon wedges.

Serves 2

spaghetti carbonara

see variations page 182

This is a sophisticated pasta dish made in the time it takes to cook the spaghetti. It does contain semi-raw eggs, which means that you shouldn't give it to anyone with a compromised immune system or who is pregnant. However, the rest of us will love its creamy texture punctuated by the saltiness of the bacon. If you want to be authentic, use Italian pancetta, otherwise, regular bacon is fine. Serve with a tomato salad.

175 g (6 oz) spaghetti
1 tsp sunflower oil
6 thin slices of bacon (preferably smoked or
   pancetta)
4 tbsp double cream

1 egg
1 egg yolk
40 g (1½ oz) Parmesan cheese, grated
black pepper, to serve

Bring a large pan of water to the boil, add the pasta and cook for about 10 minutes or as directed on the packet, until the pasta is just done (al dente).

Meanwhile, put the oil in a frying pan and spread it over the base of the pan. Add the bacon and sauté for about 3 minutes on each side until crisp. Drain on kitchen paper and, when cool enough to handle, cut into small pieces. While the bacon is cooking, beat together the cream, egg, egg yolk and 4 tbsp Parmesan cheese in a small bowl.

Drain the cooked spaghetti and return it to the hot pan (do not return it to the heat). Stir in the beaten egg mixture and bacon (reserving a little bacon for a garnish, if liked). The hot pasta will heat and thicken the sauce. Serve with the remaining Parmesan and black pepper.

Serves 2

steak with basil-garlic butter

see variations page 183

Sometimes, the old favourites are the best. This one is quick to cook and always delicious. For best results, remove the steaks from the packaging and put them on a plate in the fridge 2 hours before you start cooking, then remove the plate from the fridge 30 minutes before cooking and allow the meat to come up to room temperature.

2 lean sirloin or beef fillet steaks, about
   200–225 g (7–8 oz) each
salt

basil-garlic butter
2 tbsp salted butter, softened
2 tbsp chopped basil
1 garlic clove, finely chopped
pinch of grated lemon zest
black pepper

Preheat the grill to high. Line the grill pan with kitchen foil.

In a small bowl, stir together the butter, chopped basil, garlic, lemon zest and a good grinding of pepper.

Trim the steaks of all visible fat, then place on the lined grill pan and season with salt and pepper. Cook about 7.5 cm (3 in) away from the heat source for 1½–4 minutes on each side until done to your liking. Leave to rest in a warm place for 5 minutes before serving. This is essential as it allows the meat to relax and become more tender. Top each steak with a spoonful of the basil-garlic butter.

Serves 2

How to cook a steak

Timings are based on a sirloin steak with a thickness of about 2 cm (¾ in). Cooking times vary depending on the type and thickness of steak, and the heat intensity of the grill or pan.

Blue: 1 minute on each side.

Rare: 1½ minutes on each side.

Medium: 2¼ minutes on each side.

Medium rare: 2 minutes on each side.

Medium–well done: 2½-3 minutes on each side.

Well done: 4 minutes on each side.

tuna fish cakes

see variations page 184

If you're entertaining when money is tight, this is the recipe for you. There are variations using fresh white fish or salmon and prawns if you want a different take on the dish. Panko breadcrumbs are suggested as these produce a light and crisp crust and resist soaking up fat, but regular dry breadcrumbs would be fine, too. These fish cakes go well with chunky salsa (page 199) or mango salsa (page 208).

550 g (1¼ lb) potatoes or sweet potatoes, peeled and chopped
350 g (12 oz) can tuna in water, drained
2 spring onions, chopped
½ tsp chilli flakes
grated zest and juice of ¼ lemon

1 egg
freshly ground black pepper
100 g (3½ oz) panko breadcrumbs
3 tbsp olive oil
1 lemon, cut into wedges, to serve

Cook the potatoes or sweet potatoes in a pan of simmering water for 20 minutes. Drain well and mash. Flake the tuna and add to the potatoes with the spring onions, chilli flakes, lemon zest and juice and the egg. Season with black pepper and mix well.

Using wet hands, divide the mixture into 8 equal portions and shape into patties. Put the breadcrumbs on a plate and lightly press the fish cakes in the crumbs until coated on all sides.

Heat 2 tbsp oil in a large frying pan over a moderate heat. Sauté the fish cakes until golden on both sides. If you need to cook in batches, add the remaining oil when cooking the second batch. Serve with lemon wedges.
Serves 4

fusion chicken salad

see variations page 185

This simple salad is enlivened by a sweet, tangy dressing that completely transforms it into something magical. Look out for reduced-price rotisserie chicken pieces in the supermarket – they are displayed for a limited time, so are frequently sold off and are great for this recipe. If you want to go more Asian, use shredded pak choi instead of mixed salad greens.

salad
50 g (2 oz) flaked almonds
125 g (4 oz) chopped cooked chicken
100 g (3½ oz) mixed salad greens
1 small carrot, grated
½ red pepper, sliced
3 spring onions, sliced
parsley or coriander

dressing
1½ tbsp lime juice
1 tbsp honey
1 tbsp Thai fish sauce
2 tsp sesame oil
1 tsp soy sauce
2 tsp finely grated ginger or ginger purée
½–1 red chilli, deseeded and finely chopped,
    or ½ tsp red chilli flakes
1 garlic clove, finely chopped

Toast the flaked almonds in a hot, dry frying pan until lightly coloured. Transfer to a plate to cool. In a salad bowl toss together the remaining salad ingredients.

Put all the dressing ingredients in a small jar, screw on the lid and shake until combined. Alternatively, combine the dressing ingredients in a small bowl. When you are ready to eat, pour the dressing over the salad, toss gently to combine, then serve immediately garnished with the toasted almonds.

Serves 2

roast vegetable & feta tart

see variations page 186

A tray of roasted vegetables is a wonderful thing. It can go with simple cooked meat or chicken as a side dish; it can form the basis of a frittata or a salad; or you can serve it with couscous for a vegetarian main dish. Here we have piled the roasted vegetables into a simple tart case for a very impressive-looking main course.

1 fennel bulb, chopped
1 medium courgette, chopped
225 g (8 oz) cherry tomatoes
1 small red or yellow pepper, thickly sliced
1 small red onion, cut into wedges
1 tsp dried mixed herbs

salt and pepper
2 tbsp olive oil
1 puff pastry sheet, thawed
1 egg beaten with 1 tbsp water
2 tbsp pesto
50 g (2 oz) feta cheese, crumbled

Preheat the oven to 190°C (Gas Mark 5). Arrange the vegetables in a baking dish without overcrowding. Sprinkle over the herbs and salt and pepper, then toss lightly with the oil, coating the vegetables evenly. Roast the vegetables for 30–40 minutes, turning halfway through the cooking time. The vegetables should be tender and golden brown. Turn out onto a plate to cool.

Line a baking tray with baking paper. Unfold the pastry sheet on a lightly floured surface. Roll the pastry into a 33 x 28 cm (13 x 11 in) rectangle. Transfer the pastry to the baking tray. Brush the edges of the pastry with the beaten egg. Fold over the edges 1 cm (½ in) on all sides and press with a fork to form a rim. Prick the base of the pastry all over with a fork. Refrigerate for 30 minutes. Preheat the oven to 200°C (Gas Mark 6). Bake for 10 minutes, then use a spatula to carefully press down the puffed centre of the tart to form a shell.

Spread the pesto across the surface of the pastry. Arrange the vegetables over the top, then sprinkle with the feta cheese. Bake for about 10 minutes or until the pastry is golden brown and the cheese has melted. Serve hot or at room temperature.

Serves 4

roast chicken & potato dinner

see variations page 187

There are times when the need for this homely comfort food is overwhelming. Serve the roast chicken, potatoes and nuggets of soft garlic with your favourite vegetables.

1.3 kg (3 lb) (medium) chicken
1 lemon, halved
2 onions, quartered
10 garlic cloves
2 tbsp olive oil

salt and pepper
450 g (1 lb) new potatoes, halved
1 tsp dried mixed herbs
1 tbsp flour
350 ml (12 fl oz) good chicken stock

Preheat the oven to 190°C (Gas Mark 5).

Fill the chicken cavity with 2 lemon halves, 4 onion quarters and 2 bashed and peeled garlic cloves. Put the chicken into a large roasting pan. Using your hands, rub half the olive oil all over the chicken and season with salt and pepper. Arrange the potatoes and the remaining onion quarters and unpeeled garlic around the chicken, sprinkle with herbs and drizzle with the remaining oil, tossing the potatoes to coat.

Bake for about 1 hour and 20 minutes, basting the chicken with the juices and turning the potatoes twice. To check that the chicken is cooked, pierce the thickest part of the thigh with a skewer and press gently – the juices should run clear. Alternatively, a meat thermometer should register 74°C (165°F). Allow the chicken to rest for 15 minutes while you make the gravy, then carve into slices.

For the gravy, spoon out any visible fat from the roasting pan, then put the pan on the stove over a low heat. Stir in the flour and cook for 1 minute. Slowly add the stock, then bring to the boil, stirring constantly and scraping up the brown bits on the base of the pan. Continue to boil, reducing the liquid until it is darker and syrupy. Taste and adjust the seasoning. Pour through a sieve into a warmed gravy boat.

Serves 4

variations

prawn & coconut chowder

see base recipe page 163

coconut fish chowder

Replace the prawns with 450 g (1 lb) pollock, cod or other white fish, cut crosswise into 5 cm (2 in) wide pieces. Increase the cooking time to 5–6 minutes until the fish is cooked through.

coconut corn chowder

Add 1 medium-large potato, diced, with the coconut milk. Replace the prawns with 150 g (5 oz) frozen or canned sweetcorn and use vegetable or chicken stock. Increase the cooking time to about 10 minutes, until the sweetcorn and potatoes are tender.

old fashioned prawn chowder

Replace the coconut milk with 475 ml (16 fl oz) full-fat milk, and replace the curry paste and sugar with a dash of Worcestershire sauce. Add 1 medium-large potato, diced, with the fish stock, then add 150 g (5 oz) frozen or canned sweetcorn with the prawns. Increase the cooking time to about 10 minutes, or until the potatoes are tender. Use 6 tablespoons chopped parsley instead of coriander and basil.

coconut chicken chowder

Make the basic recipe but replace the fish stock with chicken stock and the prawns with 125 g (4 oz) chopped cooked chicken. Add 1 medium-large potato, diced, with the coconut milk and 150 g (5 oz) frozen or canned sweetcorn with the chicken. Increase the cooking time to about 10 minutes or until the sweetcorn and potatoes are tender.

variations

bruschetta with pesto & sundried tomatoes

see base recipe page 164

bruschetta with ham & red grapes
Follow the basic recipe, replacing the pesto with 1 thin slice of smoked ham or Parma ham on each side of bread and the tomato with halved red grapes. Omit the basil.

bruschetta with pâté & olives
Follow the basic recipe, replacing the pesto with your favorite pâté and replacing the tomatoes with sliced olives.

bruschetta with pesto, tomato & mozzarella
Follow the basic recipe, replacing the sundried tomato with slices of mozzarella cheese topped with slices of ripe tomato. Garnish with the basil.

bruschetta with pesto & goat's cheese
Follow the basic recipe, replacing the tomatoes on the bruschetta with slices of goat's cheese sprinkled with pepper and topped with the basil.

variations

carnivore's sharing board

see base recipe page 167

fisherman's sharing board
Replace the cold cuts with deli fish such as smoked salmon, smoked trout, anchovies, cooked prawns or seafood pâté. Serve with a side of lemon mayonnaise made from 4 tablespoons good-quality mayonnaise seasoned with ½ tablespoon lemon juice. If you have capers, use a few of these as a garnish.

vegetarian sharing board
Replace the cold cuts with antipasto such as chargrilled artichokes, roasted red and yellow peppers, mixed mushrooms, sweet peppers, sundried tomatoes and sliced mozzarella cheese.

cheese sharing board
Replace the cold cuts with a range of cheeses such as a soft herb and garlic cheese, a blue cheese, a smoked cheese, a cheese with fruit, a goat's cheese and a good sheep's cheese.

tapas sharing board
Replace the cold cuts with a selection of Spanish goodies such as sliced chorizo, cubes of Manchego cheese, deli-bought cheese-stuffed peppers, cooked prawns on a skewer with a small wedge of orange, toasted almonds and small wedges of cantaloupe melon.

variations

pork medallions with lemon & parsley

see base recipe page 168

bashed lemon chicken fillets
Replace the pork with chicken tenders (mini fillets), sliced into 2.5 cm (1 in) pieces and pounded as for the pork.

pork medallions with mushrooms
Once the pork is cooked, add 1 tablespoon each of butter and olive oil to the frying pan and cook 125 g (4 oz) sliced mushrooms, 1 finely chopped garlic clove and ½ teaspoon dried thyme, until the mushrooms are tender. Add the wine and finish as directed.

pork medallions with orange chipotle
Replace the wine and lemon juice with 175 ml (6 fl oz) orange or tangerine juice and 1–2 tablespoons chopped chipotle in adobo sauce, to taste.

pork coins with caramelised onions
Before cooking the pork, heat 1 tablespoon each of butter and olive oil in the frying pan and cook 1 large sliced onion over a moderate heat for about 5 minutes, until soft and clear, then add salt and pepper and 1 teaspoon sugar. Continue to cook, stirring frequently, for about 20 minutes until golden brown. Remove from the pan and cook the pork. Serve the pork on a bed of onions topped with the sauce.

variations

spaghetti carbonara

see base recipe page 169

spaghetti with salmon carbonara
Replace the bacon with 125 g (4 oz) smoked salmon trimmings. The salmon does not need cooking, just add it to the hot pasta.

spaghetti carbonara with lemon & chilli
Add the grated zest of ½ lemon and ½ teaspoon red chilli flakes to the egg-cream mixture.

spaghetti carbonara with garlic courgette
Increase the olive oil to 1 tablespoon and sauté 1 sliced courgette and 1 finely chopped garlic clove with the bacon. If cooking for vegetarians, omit the bacon and add grated lemon zest and chilli, as above.

spaghetti carbonara with asparagus & walnuts
Cook 125 g (4 oz) asparagus tips in the boiling water for about 3 minutes, until tender but crisp, drain with a slotted spoon and set aside. Cook the spaghetti in the same water. Omit the bacon and toast 50 g (2 oz) walnuts in the hot frying pan, without oil, for about 2 minutes, then sprinkle with a little sea salt. Proceed as directed.

variations

steak with basil-garlic butter

see base recipe page 170

steak with blue cheese butter
Make the butter by mixing together 2 tablespoons soft butter, 1 tablespoon crumbled blue cheese, ½ garlic clove, finely chopped, and ½ tablespoon chopped parsley (or ½ teaspoon dried parsley).

steak with herbed grilled tomatoes
Cut 2 ripe tomatoes in half and season with salt and pepper. Put tomatoes, cut-sides down, on a grill pan alongside the steak and cook for 3 minutes. Turn over, drizzle with a little olive oil and a pinch of dried mixed herbs, and cook for another 3 minutes. Serve with the steak.

steak with balsamic marinated mushrooms
Clean 2 portobello mushrooms and trim the stems. Marinate in a mixture of 2 tablespoons olive oil, 1 garlic clove, finely chopped, and 2 tablespoons balsamic vinegar, for 1 hour. Grill alongside the steak for about 10 minutes until cooked through.

pan-fried steaks
Heat 1 tablespoon olive oil in a frying pan over a moderate heat – the pan must be really hot. Add the steak and cook, using timings given for grilled steak (page 171), turning halfway through. Crisp the fat on the edges by tipping the steak up on its side before finishing cooking. Proceed as directed.

variations

tuna fish cakes

see base recipe page 172

fishcakes
Cook 350 g (12 oz) white fish as directed on page 70. You can choose inexpensive fish for this recipe or the meaty tails and trimmings of larger fish, such as cod and halibut, which are often sold at bargain prices. Flake the cooked fish, removing skin and bones, and proceed as directed.

salmon fishcakes with capers
Replace the tuna with 300 g (10 oz) canned pink salmon and add 1 teaspoon drained capers to the fishcake mixture.

tuna & prawn cakes
Use a 125 g (4 oz) can of prawns and reduce the tuna, fish or salmon to 175 g (6 oz).

sardine fishcakes
Use 2 x 25 g (4 oz) cans drained sardines (there's no need to remove the soft bones) and replace the chilli flakes with 1 teaspoon Dijon mustard.

fusion chicken salad

see base recipe page 173

fusion lamb salad
Omit the chicken. Pan fry a 225 g (8 oz) lamb steak in a frying pan over a moderate to high heat for 8–10 minutes until cooked. Shred the lamb; add to the salad while slightly warm.

fusion tofu salad
Cook a packet of tofu as directed on page 110. Leave to cool, then add to the salad instead of the chicken.

fusion jumbo prawns salad
Replace the chicken with 12 cooked jumbo prawns.

chicken avocado salad with lime honey dressing
Add a sliced avocado to the salad. Make the dressing from 2 tablespoons each of lime juice and olive oil, 1 tablespoon honey, 1 garlic clove, finely chopped, 1 teaspoon Dijon mustard and a pinch each of cumin, salt and black pepper.

variations

roast vegetable & feta tart

see base recipe page 174

roast vegetable & bean tart
Proceed as directed but mash a 400 g (14 oz) can white beans, rinsed and drained, with the pesto and spread over the base of the tart shell.

roast vegetable omelette
Make the omelette following the instructions on page 27. Fill with 4 tablespoons roasted vegetables.

roast vegetable pasta
Cook 350 g (12 oz) pasta. Toss the roasted vegetables with 2 tablespoons balsamic vinegar and mix into the pasta with 2 tablespoons of the pasta cooking water to moisten. Top with crumbled feta cheese.

simple plum tart
Omit the vegetables and pesto. Prepare the tart case as directed. Halve and stone 450 g (1 lb) plums, then cut into slices. Arrange in the pre-cooked pastry shell, sprinkle with 4 tablespoons caster sugar and 1 teaspoon ground cinnamon and bake as directed.

variations

roast chicken & potato dinner

see base recipe page 176

roast lamb dinner
Replace the chicken with a 1.3–1.8 kg (3–4 lb) leg of lamb. Rub the meat with oil and season as for the chicken. Put the onions into the pan with the potatoes; omit the lemon. Roast at 160°C (Gas Mark 3) for 25 minutes per 450 g (1 lb), plus 25 minutes extra, to yield a medium-cooked roast. Use lamb or beef stock for the gravy.

roast beef dinner
Replace the chicken with 900 g (2 lb) top round and bottom round beef. Rub the meat with oil and season as for the chicken. Put the onions into the pan with the potatoes; omit the lemon. Roast at 220°C (Gas Mark 7) for 20 minutes, then reduce the temperature to 190°C (Gas Mark 5) and cook for 30 minutes for rare, 40 minutes for medium or 50 minutes for well done. Make the gravy with beef stock.

roast chicken with mixed vegetables
Replace the potatoes with 675 g (1½ lb) mixed root vegetables, such as whole baby carrots, chunks of swede, chunks of celeriac, whole shallots and a few small potatoes.

chicken & artichoke tray bake
Buy or prepare chicken in joints. Put them into a baking dish with the potatoes, onions and whole garlic and 1 jar of drained artichokes. Squeeze over the juice from the lemon and add the olive oil, dried herbs and salt and pepper. Bake at 190°C (Gas Mark 5) for 45 minutes, or until the chicken is cooked though. Omit the gravy.

late night fixes

Coming home after a night out, having not eaten for hours, can present a dilemma. Often, a bowl of cereal just won't cut it – you need something substantial and tasty that's quick to cook but you have only storecupboard ingredients to fall back on. The tuna melt toastie, fish finger sandwich or shortcut mac and cheese are ideal in these circumstances. And if you're planning to come back with a group of friends, try the cowboy casserole or home-baked tortilla chips and salsa.

tuna melt toastie

see variations page 202

The perfect standby, this toastie can be served on rye bread or sourdough, but late in the evening any bread will do. No bread? See the variations to turn this recipe into a tasty pasta sauce.

2 slices of bread
2 tbsp tomato ketchup
2 tbsp mayonnaise
150 g (5 oz) can tuna, drained

4 tbsp canned sweetcorn, drained
1 tsp paprika
4 tbsp grated Cheddar cheese

Preheat the grill on a high setting.

Toast the bread on 1 side only.

Meanwhile, put all other ingredients, apart from the cheese, in a bowl and mix well.

Spread the tuna mix onto the untoasted sides of the bread, ensuring the mixture covers the bread. Sprinkle the grated cheese on top. Grill the toasties until the cheese melts and turns slightly brown. Cut in half and serve.

Serves 1

nutty banana sandwich

see variations page 203

This might not be the most fancy recipe in the world but if you are hungry and there is nothing else to hand, it's perfect. Apparently, it was also much loved by Elvis. See the variations for his favourite version (with bacon).

1 small ripe banana
2 slices of white or wholemeal bread

2 tbsp peanut butter (preferably smooth)
2 tbsp butter

Slice the banana.

Lightly toast the bread, then spread the peanut butter on 1 piece and top with the sliced banana; sandwich together.

Heat the butter in a frying pan, then cook the sandwich, turning once, until each side is golden brown.

Transfer to a plate, cut the sandwich in half and serve.

Serves 1

one-pot mac & cheese

see variations page 204

This is a clever variation on the classic. Instead of cooking the macaroni and making the cheese sauce, you cook the macaroni in the milk and the starches from the pasta thicken the milk into a smooth sauce. Add cheese and, hey presto!

225 g (8 oz) large elbow macaroni
475 ml (16 fl oz) semi-skimmed milk, plus
    extra if required
¼ tsp salt

1 tbsp butter
1 tsp Dijon mustard
125 g (4 oz) Cheddar cheese, grated
ground black pepper

Put the uncooked macaroni in a colander and quickly rinse under water, then drain. Transfer to a medium pan with the milk, salt, butter and mustard. Slowly bring the mixture to a simmer over a medium heat, stirring frequently. You need to watch carefully or the milk will boil over. Reduce the heat to low and cook the macaroni slowly in the milk, stirring from time to time.

After 15–20 minutes the macaroni will be soft and the milk will be thickened. If the mixture becomes too thick, add a little extra milk – the amount will vary depending on the brand and cooking time of the pasta.

Stir in the cheese and remove from the heat. Put the lid on the pan and leave to sit for 5 minutes to allow the macaroni to plump up and absorb any excess milk. Adjust the salt to taste and add plenty of black pepper.

Serves 2 generously

crunchy fish finger sandwich

see variations page 205

Always a winner, this nostalgic dish is now frequently found on menus in trendy cafés. It works best with good-quality soft white bread or a white roll. If two fish fingers look mean on the slice of bread, cook a couple more to fit.

2–3 fish fingers
1 tbsp butter or spread

2 slices of white bread or 1 white roll
tomato ketchup or mayonnaise

Preheat the grill on a high setting.

Grill the fish fingers until crisp and golden brown on each side, following the packet directions (usually about 5 minutes per side).

Meanwhile, butter the bread slices. Spread a little tomato ketchup or mayonnaise over 1 slice and top with the cooked fish fingers. Add more ketchup or mayonnaise over the top of the fish fingers and sandwich together with the other slice of bread. Press down gently and cut in half. Eat immediately.

Serves 1

ultimate sausage & bacon crusty roll

see variations page 206

Some people may think this is breakfast food but the dish really comes into its own late at night when you are really hungry and need a big-tasting protein and carbohydrate boost. Don't eat this every day, as it isn't the healthiest snack, but as an occasional fix, you can't beat it.

1 tbsp oil
2 small sausages
2 slices of bacon
1 large crusty roll

1 tbsp butter or spread
½ tsp Dijon mustard
tomato ketchup

Heat the oil in a frying pan over a medium heat and cook the sausages for 3 minutes. Add the bacon and continue to cook, turning occasionally, until the bacon is crisp and the sausages are nicely browned and cooked through. Make a small incision into each sausage to check that it is cooked.

Meanwhile, cut the roll in half and spread with butter followed by the mustard. Cut the sausages in half lengthwise and arrange them on the base of the roll. Top with the bacon and ketchup. This sandwich is best eaten hot.

Serves 1

swiss cheese sandwich

see variations page 207

Comfort food at its finest, this sandwich is hot, creamy and cheesy. If you want to make a meal of it, serve with some green salad leaves and a few baby tomatoes, dressed with a little balsamic vinegar.

2 thick slices of bread
about 2 tbsp butter
50 g (2 oz) grated Swiss cheese (use Gruyère
    or Emmental)

1 egg
3 tbsp milk
salt and pepper

Use about half the butter to spread on the bread, then top with the cheese and sandwich the slices of bread together.

Beat the egg with the milk in a dish that's large enough to contain the sandwich. Season with salt and pepper. Lay the sandwich in the egg mixture and leave for 5 minutes. Turn the sandwich over and repeat. By this stage, most of the egg mixture will have been absorbed.

Heat the remaining butter in a frying pan over a medium heat. Add the sandwich and cook until it has a dark golden-brown colour, then turn and cook the second side, by which time the cheese in the sandwich should have melted, too.

Serves 1

baked tortilla chips & chunky salsa

see variations page 208

This is a great sharing dish, which will keep you and your friends going while you put the world to rights. There are a selection of alternative dips in the variations section on page 208.

4 large flour tortillas (plain or with coriander and garlic)

chunky salsa
3 large tomatoes, deseeded and chopped
1 small red onion, finely chopped
1 garlic clove, finely chopped
handful of coriander, chopped
1 jalapeño pepper, finely chopped
juice of 1 lime
pinch of ground cumin
salt and pepper

Preheat the oven to 160ºC (Gas Mark 3).

Using kitchen scissors or a sharp knife, cut each tortilla into 4 or 8 wedges. Place these on a baking sheet without overlapping them and bake for 10–15 minutes, until they are crisp and slightly golden at the edges.

Meanwhile, make the salsa by combining all the ingredients together in a bowl, then adjust the seasoning to taste. Serve with the hot tortilla chips.

Serves 4

cowboy beans with hotdogs

see variations page 209

Here's another handy storecupboard standby recipe that cooks in next to no time. Serve the beans in bowls with crusty bread to mop up the yummy juices.

1 tbsp sunflower oil
1 small red onion, chopped
2 garlic cloves, finely chopped, or 2 tsp garlic
    purée
10 cm (4 in) piece of dry chorizo, sliced
½–1 tsp red chilli flakes

½ x 400 g (14 oz) can chopped tomatoes
400 g (14 oz) can baked beans
4 canned or chilled hotdogs, cut into 2 cm
    (¾ in) slices
black pepper

Heat the oil in a medium-sized pan over a moderate heat. Add the onion and cook for about 3 minutes. Add the garlic and cook for another minute, then add the chorizo slices and cook for another 4–5 minutes until the chorizo has released some of its oils. Add the chilli flakes, tomatoes and beans and cook for 5 minutes. Add the hotdogs and cook for 2 minutes to heat through. Season with pepper to taste.

Serves 2

variations

tuna melt toastie

see base recipe page 189

sicilian tuna melt
Add 4 quartered black olives, 1 tablespoon raisins and 1 teaspoon capers to the tuna mixture.

tuna pickle melt
Add 2 tablespoons chopped dill pickles and 1 tablespoon finely chopped onion to the tuna mixture.

tuna melt pasta
Cook 75 g (3 oz) pasta of your choice in boiling water until just tender. Add 4 tablespoons sour cream or milk to the tuna mixture. Stir the mixture into the hot pasta and sprinkle over the cheese.

tuna melt stuffed peppers
Cut a red or green pepper in half lengthwise and remove the seeds and membranes. Spoon the tuna mixture into the pepper halves, sprinkle with the cheese and bake at 175ºC (Gas Mark 4) for 20 minutes.

variations

nutty banana sandwich

see base recipe page 190

nutty banana bacon sandwich
Cook 2 slices of bacon in the frying pan until crisp. Remove and drain on kitchen paper, then crumble and put on top of the banana. Proceed as directed, using only 1 tablespoon butter added to the bacon fat to cook the sandwich.

chocolate banana on toast
Replace the peanut butter with Nutella or other chocolate nut spread. Or you can spread Nutella on top of the peanut butter if you prefer.

nutty banana roughie
Mash the small banana to a really smooth paste with a fork, combine with 2 tablespoons smooth peanut butter and 1 tablespoon honey. Stir in 125 ml (4 fl oz) yogurt and use the fork to thoroughly mix together. Transfer to a glass. Pour in sufficient milk (about 125 ml/ 4 fl oz) to make a thick drink. If you have a blender, blend all the ingredients together and pour into a glass. Omit the bread and butter.

healthy nutty bananas
Slice 1 big banana in half lengthwise. Combine the peanut butter with 1 tablespoon each of honey and tahini. Spread over the banana. Sprinkle with dried cranberries and mixed seeds. Omit the bread and butter.

variations

one-pot mac & cheese

see base recipe page 193

mac & cauliflower cheese
While the mac and cheese are cooking, steam the florets from half a medium cauliflower until tender. Stir into the finished mac and cheese before leaving it to rest.

jalapeño & black bean mac & cheese
Stir ½ x 400 g (14 oz) can of black beans, rinsed and drained, and 2 sliced jalapeño peppers into the finished mac and cheese before leaving it to rest.

mac & cheese with tomatoes
Stir 2 medium chopped tomatoes (preferably skinned) into the finished mac and cheese before leaving to rest.

mac & cheese with crispy bacon
While the mac and cheese are cooking, fry 4 slices of bacon until crisp. Break them into large chunks and serve over the finished mac and cheese.

variations

crunchy fish finger sandwich

see base recipe page 194

upmarket fish sandwich
Replace the tomato ketchup or mayonnaise with tartar sauce. Lay thin slices of tomato and avocado on top of the fish fingers and finish with a squeeze of lemon.

fish finger & dill pickle sandwich
Lay sliced dill pickles over the ketchup or mayonnaise on the first bread slice, then top with the fish fingers.

fish finger & cheese sandwich
Lay slices of mozzarella or Cheddar cheese on top of the ketchup or mayonnaise on the first bread slice. Grill to melt the cheese, then top with the fish fingers.

chicken nugget sandwich
Replace the fish fingers with sufficient chicken nuggets to cover the slice of bread (cook them according to package directions) and proceed as directed.

variations

ultimate sausage & bacon crusty roll

see base recipe page 196

bacon & egg sandwich
After the bacon and sausages are cooked, remove from the pan and keep warm. Fry an egg in the same pan, then add it to the bun over the sausages. And remember that eating runny egg in a bun is a messy business.

sausage & fried onion crusty roll
Omit the bacon. Cook the sausages as directed, remove them from the pan and keep warm. Drain off the excess fat and add 1 tablespoon butter. Once melted add 1 sliced small onion and a pinch of oregano. Sauté the onion until soft and beginning to brown at the edges. Make the sandwich as directed, topping the sausages with the fried onion.

herby sausage sandwich
Omit the bacon and mustard. Cook the sausage and fried onion crusty roll, as above, using herbed or paprika sausages and adding ¼ sliced red or green pepper to the onion. Also add 1 tablespoon tomato ketchup, a few drops of chilli sauce and a pinch of basil.

sausage & sauerkraut roll
Make the sausage and fried onion crusty roll above, using Polish sausage and adding 2 tablespoons prepared sauerkraut to the onion. Also add ½ teaspoon sugar, and ¼ teaspoon caraway seeds, if available.

variations

swiss cheese sandwich

see base recipe page 197

hot cheese & ham sandwich
Prepare the basic recipe, laying a slice of ham on the bread under the cheese.

simple fried cheese sandwich
Omit the egg and milk. Make the cheese sandwich without buttering the bread. Generously spread butter on the outside of 1 side of the sandwich and put it in a hot frying pan with the buttered side facing down. When golden, carefully spread butter on the other side of the sandwich, turn, then fry the second side until golden.

hot cheese & tomato sandwich
Prepare the basic recipe using thin slices of mozzarella cheese topped with slices of tomato. Either dip the sandwich in the egg mixture for a Swiss-style sandwich, or cook as above for a simple fried sandwich.

hot cheese & relish sandwich
Prepare the basic recipe, spreading the cheese filling with 1 tablespoon cranberry sauce or fruit-based chutney.

variations

baked tortilla chips & chunky salsa

see base recipe page 199

guacamole
Roughly mash the flesh from 1 large ripe avocado. Combine it with 1 large diced tomato, 1 chopped spring onion, 1 small finely chopped garlic clove and the juice of 1 lime. Add a little chilli sauce for a spicy guacamole. Season with salt and pepper and sprinkle with paprika to serve.

mango salsa
Combine the chopped flesh of 1 firm, ripe mango, ½ small chopped red onion, ½ small red chilli, deseeded and chopped, the grated zest and juice of 1 lime, a pinch of salt and 1 tablespoon chopped fresh coriander.

black bean salsa
Make the tomato salsa as directed, adding ½ x 400 g (14 oz) can black beans, rinsed and drained, with the other ingredients.

red hot salsa
Make the tomato salsa as directed but increase the number of jalapeños to 4. Add 1–2 tablespoons chilli sauce, to taste. This is good served with a side of sour cream.

variations

cowboy beans with hotdogs

see base recipe page 200

vegan cowboy beans
Use vegan sausages instead of meat-based hotdogs. Alternatively, use a packet of falafels in place of the sausages.

cowboy bean & hotdog bake
Prepare as directed and put the mixture into an ovenproof dish. At the same time, peel and slice 2 medium-large potatoes. Cook in boiling water for 5 minutes and drain. Top the casserole with potato slices, brush with a little olive oil and bake at 175°C (Gas Mark 4) for about 20 minutes until the top is golden and the potatoes are tender. This dish can be prepared ahead of time and baked when needed.

sausage & beans with leeks
Make the cowboy casserole as directed but use 2 sliced leeks instead of onions, and replace the hotdogs with good-quality cooked sausages.

chicken, bean & chorizo casserole
Make the cowboy casserole as directed but use 125 g (4 oz) diced cooked chicken or 2 cooked chicken legs instead of the hotdogs.

on the side

Many of the dishes in this book can be enhanced by a little something extra on the side. This chapter gives you a few ideas on how to use potatoes, rice and grains to bulk out a meal. It is amazing how delicious a simple potato can be when boiled and crushed with a few herbs, or oven-baked with some spices. There are also a few simple side salad and vegetable suggestions, and the ubiquitous potato salad is always a great standby.

spiced oven wedges

see variations page 225

These are delicious served as an accompaniment or on their own as a snack. Cumin and paprika work brilliantly together, but other spice combinations – such as creole spice mix, jerk spice mix or curry powder – are also excellent. Use your imagination and what you have in the cupboard. For vegans, serve with plain soy yoghurt.

2 tbsp olive oil
¼ tsp paprika
¼ tsp ground cumin
salt and pepper

2 baking potatoes (about 225 g/8 oz each)
125 ml (4 fl oz) sour cream, to serve
snipped chives (optional)

Preheat the oven to 200°C (Gas Mark 6).

Using a large baking tray, mix the oil with the paprika, cumin and a little salt and pepper. Cut each potato into 8 wedges and toss in the spiced oil to coat.

Bake for 25–30 minutes, turning once, until evenly crisp and browned. Serve with a side of sour cream and garnished with snipped chives, if liked.

Serves 2

greek salad

see variations page 226

This salad goes with just about anything and makes a change from the tired old lettuce and sliced tomato salads that appear almost everywhere. Choose the ripest tomatoes you can find and dress with the olive oil at the last minute to let the tangy tomato juices flow through the salad.

2 large ripe tomatoes, cut into chunks
⅓ cucumber, deseeded, if required, and cut into chunks
½ small red onion, very thinly sliced
1 tsp dried oregano
salt

3 tbsp olive oil
1 tsp lemon juice
black pepper
125 g (4 oz) feta cheese, crumbled
8 Greek olives, stoned

In bowl, combine the tomatoes, cucumber, onion and oregano. Sprinkle with salt to taste and leave to rest for at least 10 minutes (or up to 2 hours) so the salt can draw out the natural juices from the tomato and cucumber.

Drizzle with the olive oil and lemon juice, and sprinkle over pepper to taste. Toss the feta cheese and olives over the salad.

Serves 2

broccoli italian-style

see variations page 227

Broccoli is one of those vegetables that most people will eat, but there is a tendency to cook it to death so that it is far too soft and soggy, and tastes of cooking water. Here is a lovely way to cook it and retain its flavour. It goes well with almost everything – add a dash of soy sauce and it is good to go with an Asian dish, or a teaspoon of garam masala to turn it into a curry, or add some cooked chicken or fried tofu cubes and you have a main course. Note: If you are using frozen broccoli, omit the first step and toss it in the oil for a few minutes to cook.

225 g (8 oz) fresh broccoli, cut into 5 cm (2 in) pieces
1 tbsp olive oil
2 garlic cloves, sliced lengthwise in half

pinch of red pepper flakes
2 tsp lemon juice
salt

Put the broccoli in a microwave-safe bowl with about 2 tbsp water – there's no need to be too accurate. Cover (a plate will do) and cook on HIGH for 2 minutes. Stir to rotate the broccoli pieces, then cook for another 1–2 minutes until tender but crisp.

To cook conventionally, put the broccoli in a steamer basket in a small saucepan over 2.5 cm (1 in) water. Bring to the boil, cover and steam for 5–7 minutes or until tender but crisp.

Heat the oil in a frying pan. Cook the garlic and pepper flakes for 1–2 minutes until golden brown. Remove from the pan with a slotted spoon and discard. Add the lemon juice and a pinch of salt to the flavoured oil and pour it over the broccoli. Toss to coat, then serve.
Serves 2

potato salad

see variations page 228

This is a delicious creamy potato salad with some optional extras. If you were brought up on dill pickles in your salad, go ahead and use them, along with anything else your family favours. If you haven't got sour cream, then use all mayonnaise or Greek yogurt instead.

675 g (1½ lb) waxy potatoes such as Charlotte
1 tbsp cider vinegar or white wine vinegar
pinch of salt
3 spring onions, sliced
4 tbsp chopped fresh herbs, (parsley, chives, dill or coriander), plus extra to serve
2 celery sticks, finely chopped (optional)

4 tbsp finely chopped dill pickles or gherkins (optional)
3 tbsp sour cream or crème fraîche
3 tbsp mayonnaise
1–2 tsp Dijon or wholegrain mustard
freshly ground black pepper, to taste

Boil the potatoes in a pan of salted water, reduce the heat and simmer for about 20 minutes until just cooked. Drain, leave until cool enough to handle, then peel the potatoes.

Chop the peeled potatoes into bite-sized chunks, then put them in a large bowl. Sprinkle the vinegar over the potatoes and season lightly with salt. Toss in the spring onions and fresh herbs, plus the celery and pickles, if using. Gently stir through the sour cream, mayonnaise and mustard, and season to taste with black pepper. Leave to cool completely, then refrigerate until required, although the salad is best served at room temperature.

Serves 4 generously

french beans & bacon vinaigrette

see variations page 229

French beans are a popular vegetable to eat on the side of a main dish. This vinaigrette livens up their taste no end and turns them into something quite special. As a bonus, it works hot or at room temperature.

225 g (8 oz) French beans, trimmed
2 slices of bacon, cut into 1 cm (½ in) pieces
1 spring onion, sliced
½ tbsp cider vinegar or balsamic vinegar

½ tbsp wholegrain mustard
½ tbsp olive oil
salt and pepper

Bring a large pan of water to the boil. Add the French beans and cook for 5–6 minutes until just tender. Drain and transfer to a serving bowl and keep warm.

Meanwhile, in a medium frying pan, cook the bacon over a medium heat for 6–8 minutes until crisp.

Discard all but ½ tablespoon of the bacon fat from the frying pan and return the pan to the heat. Add the spring onion and cook for 1 minute. Stir in the vinegar, mustard and oil and season to taste with salt and pepper. Add the mixture to the French beans, along with the bacon, and toss to combine.

Serves 2

seedy couscous

see variations page 230

Nothing could be simpler or easier to cook than couscous. Serve hot with a tagine, grilled meat, chicken or fish, with stew or cold as a salad – in which case, add the spring onions and herbs once the couscous has cooled.

200 g (7 oz) couscous
½ vegetable or chicken stock cube
350 ml (12 fl oz) boiling water
4 tbsp mixed seeds

2 spring onions, sliced
4 tbsp chopped mint, parsley and/or coriander
1½ tbsp olive oil
juice of ½ lemon

Put the couscous in a heatproof bowl. Dissolve the stock cube in the boiling water, pour the stock over the couscous and stir well. Cover the bowl with a damp tea towel and leave for 5 minutes. The couscous should be soft; fluff with a fork.

Meanwhile, toast the mixed seeds in a small frying pan until just beginning to brown. Toss into the couscous with the spring onion, herbs, olive oil and lemon juice and serve hot or warm.

Serves 4

black beans & rice

see variations page 231

Beans and rice make a staple meal in cultures throughout the world. If funds are tight, this is a good dish to fall back on in its own right but it makes a tasty accompaniment too. Use whatever beans you have to hand and substitute brown rice, if you like, but remember it takes longer to cook and you will need a little extra liquid, too. In some countries, such as Cuba, hot pepper sauce, slices of mango and wedges of lime are served on the side.

1 tbsp olive oil
1 small onion, chopped
1 garlic clove, finely chopped, or
    1 tsp garlic purée
75 g (3 oz) rice
½ tsp ground cumin
pinch of chilli powder

175 ml (6 fl oz) vegetable stock, preferably
    low-salt stock
½ tsp dried oregano
½ x 400 g (14 oz) can black beans, rinsed
    and drained
2 medium tomatoes, chopped
salt and pepper

Heat the oil in a medium-sized pan over a medium heat. Add the onion and cook for 5 minutes until soft and clear. Add the garlic and cook for 1 minute. Stir in the rice, cumin and chilli, then cook for another 2 minutes until the grains of rice are translucent.

Pour in the vegetable stock and oregano, bring to the boil, reduce the heat and simmer for about 20 minutes until the rice is tender. Add the black beans and tomatoes, heat through and season to taste with salt and black pepper.

Serves 2

dhal with spinach

see variations page 232

A versatile side that goes well with any curry or vegetable dish and provides protein for a vegetarian meal. It is great, too, with rice or naan bread as an inexpensive supper. It freezes well, so bag up any leftovers for another meal. If you don't have coconut milk, don't worry, just substitute water.

200 g (7 oz) red lentils
225 ml (8 fl oz) coconut milk
475 ml (16 fl oz) cold water
¾ tsp ground turmeric
1 tsp ground cumin
½ tsp salt

2 tbsp sunflower oil
1 small onion, thinly sliced
50 g (2 oz) baby spinach or ½ teacup frozen
    spinach leaves
2 tbsp chopped coriander or parsley (optional)

Wash the lentils under cold running water, then put them in a pan with the coconut milk and water and bring to the boil. Skim off any scum with a spoon, then add the turmeric, cumin and salt. Reduce the heat and simmer, uncovered, for about 15 minutes, stirring occasionally, until the lentils have broken down and the dhal resembles porridge in texture. If the mixture gets too thick, add a little more water.

Meanwhile, heat the oil in a frying pan over a medium heat. Add the onion and sauté for 7–8 minutes until golden brown and just beginning to scorch at the edges. Stir into the cooked dhal along with the spinach and leave to sit for 5 minutes until the spinach is wilted and the flavours combined. Serve sprinkled with chopped coriander or parsley, if using.

Serves 3 as a side, 2 as a main

herby crushed potatoes

see variations page 233

Boiled potatoes can look a bit uninspiring. However, half crush them with a few herbs and some butter and they are transformed into quite a trendy side dish. Serve with any meat or fish main, or with grilled tomatoes topped with a fried egg for a simple supper.

450 g (1 lb) new potatoes such as Charlotte
2 tbsp butter or olive oil
2 tbsp snipped chives

salt
paprika, to serve (optional)

Wash the potatoes but do not peel them. Put them in a medium-sized pan, cover with cold water and bring to the boil over a medium-high heat. Reduce the heat to a simmer and cook for about 10–15 minutes or until tender. Strain and return to the pan.

Add the butter or olive oil to the pan and gently crush the potatoes with a fork or masher. Add the chives and season to taste with salt. Serve sprinkled with paprika, if liked.

Serves 3–4

variations

spiced oven wedges

see base recipe page 211

spiced sweet potato wedges
Follow the basic recipe, using sweet potatoes instead of baking potatoes.

lemon thyme oven wedges
Replace the cumin with the juice of 1 lemon and 1 teaspoon dried thyme.

crispy oven wedges
Omit the paprika and cumin. Using salt flakes or roughly ground sea salt is a nice touch. Serve with mayonnaise or sour cream, if liked.

parmesan-loaded oven wedges
Omit the cumin and add 2 tablespoons grated Parmesan cheese to the spice mixture. Cook as directed. For a decadent touch, when cooked, toss in another 2 tablespoons grated Parmesan, mixed with 1 tablespoon chopped parsley. Serve drizzled with sour cream and topped with bacon bits.

variations

greek salad

see base recipe page 212

loaded greek main course salad
Make the greek salad as directed. Add ½ x 400 g (14 oz) can chickpeas, rinsed and drained, 1 small chopped green pepper, 2 tablespoons toasted whole almonds and 1 teaspoon capers to the salad. Sit the salad on a bed of torn lettuce.

greek salad pitta
Make the salad as directed. Toast a pitta bread in the toaster until soft and puffed out. Cut in half and carefully separate the top and bottom layers of the pitta to make a pocket. Fill with the salad.

fishy greek salad
Make the greek salad as directed and top with the well drained sardines from a 85 g (3 oz) can.

greek salad with grape leaves & artichokes
Add 8 sliced sweet pickled peppers to the salad and top with 6 stuffed grape leaves and 2 marinated artichoke hearts. The ingredients can be from jars or bought from the deli counter.

variations

broccoli italian-style

see base recipe page 215

pasta with lemon broccoli
Increase the oil to 2 tablespoons. Toss the broccoli through 2 portions of cooked pasta (about 175 g/6 oz uncooked). Add Parmesan shavings to serve.

broccoli with sundried tomatoes & olives
Add 2 tablespoons chopped sundried tomatoes and 6 halved black stoned olives to the hot oil. Cook for 1 minute to heat through before tossing in the broccoli. This is also good served over pasta.

soy & honey broccoli
Add 1 teaspoon ginger purée with the garlic. Replace the lemon with 1 tablespoon soy sauce and 1 teaspoon runny honey.

french beans italian-style
Replace the broccoli with 225 g (8 oz) French beans. Microwave or steam as for the broccoli. Proceed as directed adding 1 medium chopped tomato (for finesse, skinned and deseeded).

variations

potato salad

see base recipe page 216

warm german potato salad
Cook 4 slices of smoked bacon in a large frying pan over a medium-high heat until crisp and brown. Remove from the pan, crumble and set aside. Stir 1 tablespoon plain flour into the bacon fat in the frying pan, then add 1 tablespoon sugar, 90 ml (3 fl oz) water and 4 tablespoons vinegar to the frying pan and cook until the dressing is thick. Add the bacon, potatoes, onion and parsley, stir until warm, then serve immediately. Omit the remaining ingredients.

potato, olive & tomato salad
Prepare the basic potato salad, adding 12 stoned olives and 2 medium tomatoes, cut into chunks.

lemony light potato salad
Replace the sour cream and mayonnaise with 2 tablespoons each of olive oil and lemon juice and the grated zest of ½ lemon.

curried mayonnaise potato salad
Replace the sour cream with low-fat natural yogurt. Mix 1–2 teaspoons medium curry powder, ½ tablespoon mango chutney or cranberry sauce, and 1 teaspoon red chilli flakes into the mayonnaise. Use to dress the potato salad. Omit the dill pickles.

variations

french beans & bacon vinaigrette

see base recipe page 218

french beans & tomato vinaigrette
Omit the bacon. Heat the olive oil in a small pan and cook the spring onion for 1 minute.
Add 1 chopped (preferably skinned) tomato, the vinegar and the mustard. Proceed as
directed.

french beans with lemon & almonds
Omit the bacon and vinegar. Heat the olive oil in a small pan and cook the spring onion for
1 minute. Add the juice of 1 lemon and the mustard and heat through. Proceed as for the
basic recipe. Serve scattered with 2 tablespoons toasted flaked almonds.

pasta with creamy french beans & bacon
Replace the vinegar with 2 tablespoons sour cream or Greek yogurt, 1 tablespoon milk
and 2 tablespoons pasta cooking water. Toss into 2 portions cooked pasta (about 175 g/6 oz
uncooked) and serve with grated Parmesan cheese.

cabbage & bacon vinaigrette
Cook the bacon as directed and remove it from the pan. Add ½ small sliced onion to the
bacon fat, plus the olive oil, and sauté for 5 minutes until soft. Add ½ small white cabbage,
shredded, 2 tablespoons water and a pinch each of sugar, salt and pepper. Cook for about
15 minutes until the cabbage wilts. Stir in the bacon, vinegar and mustard and heat through.

variations

seedy couscous

see base recipe page 219

couscous with tomatoes
Cook the couscous in the stock as directed; omit the mixed seeds. While the couscous is resting add 2 medium chopped tomatoes (preferably deseeded and skinned.) If serving as a salad, add the tomatoes with the other ingredients after the couscous has cooled.

spicy couscous & chickpeas
Add 1/3 x 400 g (14 oz) can chickpeas, rinsed and drained, to the uncooked couscous. Stir 1/2 teaspoon harissa into the water with the stock and proceed as directed. If you haven't got harissa, use chilli sauce instead.

couscous & feta fritters
Add 50 g (2 oz) crumbled feta cheese, 1/2 beaten egg and 1½ tablespoons yogurt to the cooked and cooled couscous. Divide the mixture into 4 equal portions and shape into burgers. Heat 1 tablespoon olive oil in a frying pan, then cook over a medium heat for 3 minutes on each side until golden.

tabbouleh
Replace the couscous with bulgur wheat and allow to stand for 1 hour. Add all the other ingredients except the seeds. Also add 1 large chopped tomato (preferably deseeded and skinned) and 10 cm (4 in) piece of chopped cucumber. This dish is good served with pan-seared halloumi (page 150).

black beans & rice

see base recipe page 221

mexican beans & rice
When adding the cumin power also add 1 chopped jalapeño pepper and 1 tablespoon tomato purée.

coconut rice & beans
Replace 90 ml (3 fl oz) of the vegetable stock with reduced-fat coconut milk and add ½–1 teaspoon red chilli flakes.

quick jambalaya
Cook 175 g (6 oz) sliced Spanish, Polish or other spiced or smoked sausage and ½ green pepper, chopped, in the oil with the onion. Replace the cumin with 1 teaspoon Cajun spices, if available. Stir 8 large cooked prawns into the rice instead of the beans.

rice & lentils
Replace the beans with ½ x 400 g (14 oz) can green lentils, rinsed and drained, or 200 g (7 oz) freshly cooked green lentils. This makes a good cold salad base, as well as a hot side dish.

dhal with spinach

see base recipe page 222

dhal with chickpeas
Stir ½ x 400 g (14 oz) can chickpeas, rinsed and drained, into the almost-cooked dhal and heat through, then proceed as directed.

tomato dhal
Add 1 teaspoon tomato purée with the coconut milk and water, then add 2 medium chopped tomatoes with the spinach to heat through. Proceed as directed.

spicy lemon dhal
Add 1 chopped red chilli (deseeded for a milder flavour) to the onions about 2 minutes before they are cooked. Once cooked, stir in the grated zest and juice of ½ lemon and proceed as directed.

dhal with egg
For an inexpensive supper make the dhal and top with 1 fried egg or 1 hard-boiled egg, peeled and cut into quarters (page 47).

variations

herby crushed potatoes

see base recipe page 224

crushed potatoes with grainy mustard
Replace the chives with 1–2 tablespoons grainy mustard, to taste.

garlic crushed potatoes
Add 2 whole garlic cloves when cooking the potatoes. When drained, remove the skin and mash to a paste with a fork. Return to the pan when crushing the potatoes. Garnish with chives or chopped fresh parsley.

mashed potatoes
Replace the salad potatoes with floury potatoes, such as King Edwards, cut into large pieces. Cook in the boiling water for about 20 minutes until very tender, but not disintegrating. Mash until smooth with a potato masher (do not be tempted to use a blender or you will end up with a glue-like texture). Add the butter and salt plus 3–4 tablespoons milk or single cream for a rich, creamy texture. Stir through the chives and garnish with paprika.

chunky colcannon
While the potatoes are cooking, cook 3 slices of bacon until crisp. Remove from the pan and chop into pieces. Shred ¼ small green cabbage. Add the butter to the bacon fat and sauté the cabbage until just tender. Crush the potatoes as directed and stir in the bacon and cabbage and 90 ml (3 fl oz) warmed single cream. Season with salt and pepper. Omit the paprika and chives.

something sweet

Few people can resist dessert and the recipes here
are shamelessly fun and enjoyable. Still, it is best to
avoid eating ice cream, cheesecake and chocolate
fondue on a daily basis. That isn't to say that
healthy eating can't be pleasurable eating – the
chargrilled pineapple, the spiced oranges and dates,
and the summer berry crisp are sensible choices
while still being delectable.

white chocolate strawberry cheesecake

see variations page 251

This cheat's cheesecake requires no baking and can be served either as soon as it is made or kept covered in the fridge for a few hours, or overnight.

4 digestive biscuits
8 strawberries, chopped
75 g (3 oz) cream cheese
2 tbsp icing sugar
¼ tsp vanilla extract

¼ tsp lemon juice
90 ml (3 fl oz) double cream or Greek yogurt
1 square of white chocolate, grated

Put the biscuits in a plastic bag and crush them until they are chunky crumbs. Divide them equally between 2 glasses and press down lightly.

Reserve 1 strawberry for decoration and roughly chop the remainder. Divide the chopped strawberries between the 2 glasses.

Beat together the cream cheese, icing sugar, vanilla, lemon juice and cream until thick. Top each glass with the mixture followed by the grated chocolate. Cut the remaining strawberry in half and use to garnish each cheesecake.

Serves 2

pears with ice cream & hot chocolate sauce

see variations page 252

This is a quick version of the classic dessert Pears Belle Helene. The chocolate sauce is deliciously rich, thanks to the evaporated milk, and because the pears are from a can, this is a handy recipe to have up your sleeve when you need a storecupboard pudding.

4 canned pear halves
2–4 scoops of vanilla ice cream

chocolate sauce
75 g (3 oz) dark chocolate chips
1 tbsp butter
½ x 400 g (14 oz) can evaporated milk
1 tbsp caster sugar
½ tsp vanilla extract
1 tbsp water

In a saucepan, combine all the sauce ingredients. Slowly bring to a simmer and cook, stirring, until the chocolate has melted and the ingredients are well combined.

Arrange the pears, 1 tbsp of the pear juice and the ice cream in 2 dishes and pour over the hot chocolate sauce.

Serves 2

nutty chocolate mousse

see variations page 253

Serve this deliciously rich dessert in small teacups, glasses or espresso cups. If you like your mousse light and airy, you could, after adding the cream, fold in an egg white that has been beaten until lightly stiffened; remember the usual health advice for eating raw egg (page 88).

125 g (4 oz) good quality dark chocolate
225 ml (8 fl oz) double cream
2 tbsp water

50 g (2 oz) mini marshmallows, plus
  a few extra to garnish
2 tbsp smooth peanut, almond or
  other nut butter

Put the chocolate, 125 ml (4 fl oz) of the cream, the water, marshmallows and peanut butter in a dry, heatproof bowl set over a pan of simmering water. Take care not to allow the base of the bowl to make contact with the water beneath it, in the pan. Stir the mixture until smooth and melted, then remove the bowl from the heat and leave to cool to room temperature. (You can accelerate the cooling process by sitting the bowl in cold water.)

Beat the remaining cream with a wire whisk until soft peaks form. Carefully fold the cream into the cooled chocolate mixture using a spatula or large metal spoon. Pour into bowls and chill for at least 2 hours before serving decorated with a few marshmallows.

Serves 3

ice box minis

see variations page 254

This is an indulgent no-cook recipe that should be rested overnight in the fridge – you better do a good job of hiding it, though! The finished result is always a delight and is a sure-fire winner every time. Choose biscuits with a diameter of about 5 cm (2 in) to give a good-sized portion. Other good biscuit choices include digestives, double chocolate chip biscuits and shortbread.

225 ml (8 fl oz) double cream
1 tbsp icing sugar
½ tsp vanilla extract

2 packets of chocolate chip biscuits
chocolate chips, M&Ms or other sweets, to decorate

Beat the cream and icing sugar together with a wire whisk until soft peaks form, then stir in the vanilla. Do not over beat – the cream should still be floppy and light.

Put 1 biscuit on a large plate. Drop a rounded tsp of whipped cream onto the centre of the biscuit and flatten, leaving a rim of about 3 mm (⅛ in) around the outside edge of the biscuit. Gently press another biscuit on top of the whipped cream until the cream is flush with the edges. Continue until you have stacked 6 biscuits to make 1 mini cake. Finish off with a layer of whipped cream. Repeat until the cream and biscuits are used up – you should make 5 mini cakes.

Chill in the fridge for at least 6 hours, but preferably overnight, to allow the liquid from the cream to seep into the biscuits. Just before serving, decorate with chocolate chips, M&Ms or sweets of your choice.

Makes about 5

almost-instant chocolate chip ice cream

see variations page 255

This ice cream is almost a science lesson in itself. It is handmade in every sense, given that the best way to chill it is to pass it from person to person to keep it churning! Tips for success: have thick plastic freezer bags that will not tear and seal the zip-lock bags thoroughly (one leak and your efforts are in vain). Better still, secure the seal with parcel tape as well. And wear warm gloves!

225 ml (8 fl oz) full cream milk
1 tbsp caster or icing sugar
½ tsp vanilla extract
30 g (1 oz) good chocolate, cut into chips

6 tbsp salt
about 450 g (1 lb) ice
ice cream sprinkles or chopped nuts (optional)

Double up 2 medium-sized zip-lock bags and put them in a bowl. Pour the milk, sugar, vanilla and chocolate chips into the doubled bag and seal tightly.

Take a large zip-lock bag and add the salt and half fill with ice. Put the doubled-up medium bag into the larger bag, then seal this bag, too. Wearing gloves, pass the parcel around from person to person to freeze the ice cream – this will take up to 15 minutes. If working on your own, put the salt, ice and bags with the milk mixture in a plastic container and keep them moving around.

Serve the frozen ice cream decorated with ice cream sprinkles or chopped nuts, if liked.
Serves 2

chargrilled pineapple

see variations page 256

This is an easy storecupboard dessert that is utterly delicious with a scoop of ice cream or a little Greek yogurt. It works well for breakfast, too – without the ice cream!

4 pineapple slices
2 tsp butter, softened
2 tbsp brown sugar

¼ tsp ground cinnamon or 4 pinches
    of ground ginger

Put the pineapple slices on a grill pan. Spread each slice with about ½ tsp butter, then sprinkle over the brown sugar and cinnamon or ginger.

Position the pineapple slices about 10 cm (4 in) away from the heat and grill on one side only for about 5 minutes, until bubbling and the sugar is just beginning to take on a dark brown caramelised colour.

Serves 2

spiced orange & date salad

see variations page 257

A refreshing fruit salad that brings the flavours of Morocco to your table. The oranges are served in a simple syrup that can be adapted and used for other fruits, making this a versatile recipe, too. Traditionally, a little orange flower water would be added to the syrup but this is not essential. However, if you happen to have some, it adds a touch of authenticity.

syrup
4 tbsp granulated sugar
1 tbsp lemon juice
3 tbsp water
¼ tsp ground cinnamon

salad
2 tbsp flaked almonds
2–3 medium oranges, peeled and sliced
100 g (3½ oz) chopped stoned dates

Combine the syrup ingredients in a medium-sized saucepan. Bring to the boil, stirring, until the sugar has dissolved. Allow to cool.

Meanwhile, heat a medium-sized frying pan and toast the almonds, stirring frequently, until lightly golden. Set aside to cool.

Put the orange slices in a bowl and pour over the cooled syrup. Add the dates, then leave to stand for about 30 minutes to infuse. Sprinkle over the toasted almonds to serve.

Serves 2

summer berry crisp

see variations page 258

This is such a homely dessert and surprisingly easy to cook as well. It's made with frozen fruit, which is more convenient and easier to store; however, use fresh berries if you have some that needs using up.

fruit base
325 g (12 oz) packet of frozen mixed berries,
    unthawed
2 tbsp light brown sugar
1 tbsp plain flour
1 tsp lemon juice

crisp topping
6 tbsp light brown sugar
6 tbsp uncooked porridge oats
4 tbsp plain flour
pinch of fine salt
½ tsp ground cinnamon
3 tbsp chilled butter, cut into small pieces

Preheat the oven to 190°C (Gas Mark 5). Grease a small ovenproof dish with butter.

To make the fruit base, combine the ingredients in a bowl and toss to mix. Pour the berry mixture into the prepared ovenproof dish.

For the crisp topping, combine the brown sugar, oats, flour, salt and cinnamon in a bowl until evenly mixed. With your fingertips, blend in the butter pieces until the mixture forms small clumps and the butter is well incorporated.

Sprinkle the topping evenly over the berries and bake for 50–60 minutes until the topping is crispy. Cool on a rack for at least 30 minutes before serving warm, or leave to cool to room temperature before serving.
Serves 3–4

greek yogurt with warm blueberry sauce

see variations page 259

This is another versatile recipe that can be adapted to suit your mood and the contents of your fridge. If serving for friends, put it into tall glasses and serve with shortbread or another butter-rich biscuit for an elegant touch.

100 g (3½ oz) blueberries
4 tbsp water
2 tbsp sugar

1 tbsp lemon juice
½ tbsp butter
225 ml (8 fl oz) fat-free Greek yogurt

Combine the blueberries, water, sugar and lemon juice in a small pan and slowly bring to the boil. Simmer over a low heat for about 6 minutes or until the sauce thickens. Stir in the butter, then take the pan off the heat and leave to stand for a few minutes until the mixture has cooled slightly.

Divide the yogurt between 2 bowls or glasses and pour over the warm sauce. Swirl with a knife to create a marbled effect.

Alternatively, make the sauce ahead of time and allow to cool completely, then serve it as a cold dessert.

Serves 2

apple strudel

see variations page 260

Using frozen puff pastry makes this dessert simple to make and it looks very impressive, too. It is one of those recipes that, once tried, will be revisited many times over the years. Serve with lightly whipped cream or with vanilla ice cream.

1 sheet of puff pastry, thawed if frozen
2 large Granny Smith or Cox's apples, peeled,
   cored and thinly sliced
juice of ½ lemon
50 g (2 oz) light brown sugar

4 tbsp raisins
1 tsp ground cinnamon
1 tbsp milk
2 tbsp flaked almonds or chopped mixed nuts
1 tbsp icing sugar

Preheat the oven to 200°C (Gas Mark 6).

Carefully unroll the pastry and place it on a sheet of baking paper or an ungreased baking sheet.

Put the sliced apple into a bowl and add the lemon juice, sugar, raisins and cinnamon; toss to mix. Pile the apple mixture into the centre of the pastry sheet. Dampen the edges of the pastry with water. Gently bring the 2 long edges together and seal tightly. Fold in the 2 short ends and press to seal. Check all the seals to ensure there are no holes. Make a few slits in the top of the pastry to allow the steam to escape.

Brush the top with milk and sprinkle over the nuts. Bake for 15–20 minutes until golden brown. Dust with sifted icing sugar and serve either warm or at room temperature.
Makes 4–6 slices

microwave vanilla fudge

see variations page 261

It is good to have a simple recipe for fudge for those times when nothing but sugar will do. Fudge also makes an inexpensive gift and everybody appreciates something that has been thoughtfully and lovingly made. Wrap in clear plastic and decorate flamboyantly with a ribbon bow for the best effect.

125 g (4 oz) butter, cut into pieces
225 g (8 oz) caster sugar

400 g (14 oz) can condensed milk
1 tsp vanilla extract

Line an 20 cm (8 in) square baking tin or foil container with baking paper.

Put the butter in the largest microwave-safe glass bowl that you have (plastic might melt). Cook the butter on HIGH in 30 second-intervals until melted. Stir in the sugar and pour in the condensed milk. Cook on HIGH for about 10 minutes, stopping every minute to stir. The cooked fudge will be golden brown. If you have a sugar thermometer it should read 113–116°C (235–240°F). To check if it is ready by sight, a small amount of fudge dropped into chilled water forms a soft ball that flattens after a few seconds in your hand.

Leave to cool for 5 minutes, stir in the vanilla, then beat with a wooden spoon until the fudge starts to set and loses its shine. Pour the mixture into the prepared tin and leave to set before cutting into squares.

Makes about 36 pieces

white chocolate strawberry cheesecake

see base recipe page 235

chocolate orange cheesecake in a glass
Replace the digestive biscuits with chocolate biscuits. Use only a few drops of vanilla and replace the lemon juice with 1 teaspoon orange juice and 1 teaspoon orange zest. Replace the strawberries with the chopped flesh of ½ orange. Replace the white chocolate with orange-flavoured chocolate.

strawberry granola cheesecake in a glass
Replace the digestive biscuits with 2 tablespoons granola per glass. Omit the white chocolate and sprinkle more muesli over the top of the glass before decorating the cream-cheese mixture with the halved strawberries.

raspberry ginger cheesecake in a glass
Replace the digestive biscuits with ginger biscuits and the strawberries with raspberries. Also, replace the white chocolate with ginger-flavoured chocolate.

dairy-free strawberry lemon cheesecake in a glass
Use vegan or dairy-free biscuits and make the cheesecake with soy-based vegan cream cheese and vegan chocolate.

variations

pears with ice cream & hot chocolate sauce

see base recipe page 236

pineapple with hot chocolate sauce
Replace the pears with 4 slices of fresh or canned pineapple. Serve with the hot chocolate sauce. Omit the ice cream.

madeira cake fondue
Make the chocolate sauce and pour it into a bowl. Cut cubes of Madeira cake and arrange on a plate with 2 forks. Dip the cake into the hot sauce and eat immediately. This is delicious with chocolate cake too!

banana split with hot chocolate sauce
Make the chocolate sauce. Replace the pears with a small banana. Pour the chocolate sauce over the banana and ice cream and serve scattered with a few toasted flaked almonds.

chocolate nut sundae
Make the chocolate sauce, adding 4 tablespoons smooth peanut butter. In a sundae or tall glass, put 1 scoop of toffee ice cream, followed by a scoop of chocolate ice cream. Pour over the hot chocolate sauce and sprinkle over some chopped peanuts or pecans.

variations

nutty chocolate mousse

see base recipe page 239

chocolate mousse
Omit the peanut butter. Add ¼ teaspoon vanilla extract to the cooled chocolate mixture.

easy layered chocolate mousse
Replace the cream with evaporated milk and use 75 g (3 oz) mini marshmallows. Omit the peanut butter. When beating the evaporated milk it will become frothy and stiff. Fold it into the cooled chocolate mixture without over-mixing – that way, the mousse separates into a creamy bottom layer and an airy top layer. Omit the peanut butter.

mocha mousse
Replace the water with 2 tablespoons strong coffee, preferably espresso.

minty mousse
Omit the peanut butter. Add a few drops of peppermint extract for a stronger flavour or crushed mints for texture.

chocolate mousse tart
Buy a pastry tart shell and fill with the nutty chocolate mousse. Garnish with white and plain chocolate shavings.

variations

ice box minis

see base recipe page 240

mocha ice box minis
Replace the vanilla with 1 tablespoon strong coffee, preferably espresso, and 25 g (1 oz) melted plain chocolate.

chocolate chilli ice box minis
Replace the vanilla with 25 g (1 oz) melted plain chocolate, 1–2 teaspoons chilli powder and ¼–½ teaspoon cayenne pepper. Add the chilli powder a little at a time until the mixture is spicy enough for you.

strawberry chocolate ice box minis
Add 10 finely chopped strawberries to the whipped cream. Decorate with strawberry slices instead of chocolate chips or sweets.

mango ginger ice box minis
Replace the chocolate chip biscuits with ginger biscuits. Add 3 tablespoons finely chopped mango (fresh or canned) to the whipped cream. Decorate with mango slices.

variations

almost-instant chocolate chip ice cream

see base recipe page 241

vanilla handmade ice cream
Omit the chocolate chips.

chocolate handmade ice cream
Add 2 tablespoons chocolate sauce or Nutella to the milk in the bag.

blueberry handmade ice cream
Add 75 g (3 oz) frozen blueberries to the milk in the bag.

honeycomb handmade ice cream
Replace the chocolate with 50 g (2 oz) honeycomb or Crunchie bar, broken into pieces, and replace the sugar with honey. Serve with more honeycomb.

lemon handmade ice cream
Reduce the vanilla to a few drops. Add the grated zest and juice of ½ lemon to the bag with the milk. Increase the sugar to 2 tablespoons.

variations

chargrilled pineapple

see base recipe page 242

chargrilled mango
Cut down both sides of 2 mangoes without removing the peel. Proceed as directed, serving with a squeeze of lime juice.

chargrilled banana
Peel 2 bananas and rub each with about 1 teaspoon lemon juice. Omit the butter. Simply sprinkle with brown sugar and cinnamon or ginger. Grill as directed for 4 minutes, then turn the bananas over and grill for a further 3–4 minutes until soft.

chargrilled peaches
Halve and stone 2 ripe peaches. Prepare and cook as directed.

chargrilled grapefruit
Halve 1 large pink or white grapefruit. If you cut beside the membranes of the grapefruit to segment, and around the inner pith, it will be much easier to eat. Prepare and cook as directed. Omit the cinnamon and ginger.

variations

spiced orange & date salad

see base recipe page 245

quick orange & date salad
Omit the syrup and pour 4 tablespoons orange and mango juice over the fruit and sprinkle with ground cinnamon.

spiced orange, date & pomegranate salad
Add the seeds of ¼ small pomegranate with the dates.

spiced peaches & dates
Replace the oranges with 2 large peaches, peeled, stoned and sliced. (To peel, submerge the peach in boiling water for 20 seconds, run under cold water to cool, then peel off the skin.)

minted oranges & strawberries
Add 8 sliced strawberries to the oranges and use 1 tablespoon chopped fresh mint instead of the cinnamon.

variations

summer berry crisp

see base recipe page 246

apple crisp

Replace the berries with 3 large Granny Smith or 2 medium cooking apples, peeled, cored and cut into 5 mm (¼ in) slices. Also add ½ teaspoon ground cinnamon to the fruit. Make the topping and proceed as directed.

apple & pear crisp

Replace the berries with 2 large Granny Smith or 1 large cooking apple and 1 medium pear, all peeled, cored and cut into 5 mm (¼ in) slices. Also add ½ teaspoon ground cinnamon to the fruit.

minted berry with nutty crisp

Add 1 teaspoon dried mint or 1 tablespoon chopped fresh mint to the berries. Also add 2 tablespoons flaked almonds and 1 tablespoon sunflower seeds to the crisp.

peach & blueberry crisp

Replace the berries with a 400 g (14 oz) can peach halves in natural juices, drained, and 75 g (3 oz) fresh or frozen blueberries. Also add ½ teaspoon ground cinnamon to the base. Make the topping and proceed as directed.

greek yogurt with warm blueberry sauce

see base recipe page 247

ice cream with warm raspberry sauce
Replace the blueberries with raspberries and serve over raspberry ripple ice cream.

waffles with warm blueberry sauce
Toast 4 Belgian waffles following the package directions. Serve with warm blueberry sauce and 4 tablespoons Greek yogurt or lightly whipped cream.

double blueberry pancakes
Make the blueberry oat pancakes (page 17) and serve with the warm blueberry sauce.

blueberry & strawberry parfait
Make the blueberry sauce and leave to cool completely. Put 1 tablespoon muesli in the base of a tall glass. Add a layer of blueberry sauce, then a layer of yogurt; repeat. Put a layer of sliced strawberries on top of the final layer of yogurt.

variations

apple strudel

see base recipe page 248

apple & blackberry strudel
Use only 1½ apples and replace the raisins with 150 g (5 oz) blackberries.

sweet cheese strudel
Omit the apple filling. In a bowl combine 125 g (4 oz) each of cream cheese and fromage frais or ricotta cheese, both at room temperature. Beat in 1 egg, 125 g (4 oz) caster sugar and 1 teaspoon vanilla extract. Stir in 4 tablespoons raisins. Construct the strudel as directed.

french apple tart
Prepare the pastry as directed. Core, then slice, 4 unpeeled red Cox's apples and toss in the lemon juice. Slightly overlap the apple slices in rows on top of the pastry, leaving a 5 cm (2 in) gap around the edges. Drizzle 2 tablespoons melted butter over the apples, sprinkle with 4 tablespoons caster sugar and dust with cinnamon. Brush the pastry edges with milk and fold the edges inwards, pressing down to form a crust. Bake as directed.

apple sauce
Combine the apples, lemon, sugar and cinnamon in a medium pan. Cook over a moderate heat, stirring often, until the apples are tender but holding their shape. For a smooth apple sauce, cook for a little longer and beat with a wooden spoon until puréed.

variations

microwave vanilla fudge

see base recipe page 250

sour cherry fudge
Add 65 g (2½ oz) chopped sour cherries just before pouring the fudge into the prepared tin.

coconut fudge
Add 3 tablespoons desiccated or shredded coconut with the vanilla.

chocolate fudge
Add 3 tablespoons cocoa powder to the sugar when cooking the fudge.

pecan fudge
Add 75 g (3 oz) chopped pecans just before pouring the fudge into the prepared tin.

stove-top fudge
Put the ingredients into a large non-stick saucepan and melt over a low heat, stirring until the sugar dissolves. Bring to the boil, then simmer for 10–15 minutes, stirring continuously with a wooden spoon to prevent the fudge from sticking and burning at the base and in the corners of the pan. Take care – the mixture is very hot. Test and finish as directed.

a bit of baking

Baking can be a fun and sociable activity and the
end result makes you friends! These recipes are
selected for their ease and reliability. Presumably,
student accommodation doesn't provide food
mixers, so beating is done by hand – not a problem
with the brownies and muffins, and the birthday
cake contains oil, reducing the need for vigorous
beating. You still get an arm-muscle workout but
only a mini one. To really cheat, make the tiffin – it
requires no baking and is ridiculously moreish.

fudgy brownies

see variations page 276

This is a classic. The trick with brownies is not to over-bake them; you need to take them out of the oven as soon as they pull away from the sides of the pan, while the centre is still soft. Served warm, they are delicious as a dessert with a few strawberries and some ice cream, but they are equally tempting eaten cold with a glass of milk.

65 g (2½ oz) butter	2 eggs
125 g (4 oz) plain chocolate	½ tsp vanilla extract
225 g (8 oz) caster sugar	75 g (3 oz) self-raising flour

Preheat the oven to 175°C (Gas Mark 4). Grease a 20 x 20 cm (8 x 8 in) cake tin and line it with baking paper.

Put the butter and chocolate in a medium-sized pan and melt over a low heat, stirring occasionally. Remove from the heat. Using a wooden spoon, beat in the sugar, eggs and vanilla. Stir in the flour.

Pour the batter into the prepared tin and bake for 25–30 minutes until the edges and top are set but the mixture feels soft underneath. Cool for 15 minutes, then slice into bars and remove from the pan. Finish cooling on a wire rack.

Makes 9 or 12 bars

vanilla birthday cake

see variations page 277

Having a celebration cake recipe is a must for everyone. What nicer present could you give to a friend than a personalised birthday cake? You can customise the decorations to suit their personality and add a candle or two for effect. However, don't save this recipe for special occasions – it is lovely to eat at any time.

225 g (8 oz) caster sugar
4 eggs
300 g (10 oz) self-raising flour
175 ml (6 fl oz) sunflower oil
150 ml (¼ pint) milk
1½ tsp vanilla extract
sprinkles or other cake decorations, to decorate

icing
350 g (12 oz) icing sugar, sifted
65 g (2½ oz) butter, at room temperature
1½ tsp vanilla extract
about 2 tbsp milk

Preheat the oven to 175ºC (Gas Mark 4). Line two 23 cm (9 in) round cake tins or one 33 x 23 cm (13 x 9 in) tin with baking paper. Grease the paper and the sides of the pan with a little oil or butter.

In a large mixing bowl and with a wire whisk, beat the sugar and eggs together for 4–5 minutes (or about 1 minute with a food mixer) until slightly thickened. Add the flour, oil, milk and vanilla and beat until the batter is smooth and creamy. Pour the batter into the prepared baking tins.

Bake for 30–35 minutes for the round cakes, 35–40 minutes for the oblong cake; the tops should be golden and a cocktail stick inserted into the centre of the cake should come out

clean. Rest for 5 minutes. Loosen the sides of the cake from the tin using a knife, then turn out onto a wire rack and peel off the paper. Cool completely before covering with the icing.

To make the icing, mix the icing sugar and butter together with a soft spatula or spoon. Stir in the vanilla and sufficient milk to give the mixture a spreadable consistency. Spread just under half the icing over the top of one cake, top with the other layer and spread the remaining icing over the top. Decorate with sprinkles or other cake decorations.

Serves 2

cranberry flapjacks

see variations page 278

A flapjack is a wonderful thing to eat as a snack and, being quite dense, it is easy to transport, sealed in a little clingfilm. What's more, it costs a fraction of those fancy flapjacks served in coffee shops and it couldn't be simpler to make.

125 g (4 oz) butter or dairy-free spread
225 g (8 oz) light brown sugar
3 tbsp golden syrup, maple syrup or thick honey

175 g (6 oz) porridge oats
50 g (2 oz) dried cranberries
3 tbsp pumpkin seeds

Preheat the oven to 175ºC (Gas Mark 4). Grease an 20 x 20 cm (8 x 8 in) cake tin and line it with baking paper.

Put the butter, sugar and golden syrup in a medium-sized pan and melt over a low heat, stirring occasionally. Remove from the heat and stir in the porridge oats, cranberries and pumpkin seeds.

Pour the mixture into the prepared tin and bake for 15–20 minutes until just beginning to turn golden – do not over-cook. Cool for 5 minutes, then slice into bars and remove from the tin. Finish cooling on a wire rack.

To cook in the microwave: put the butter, sugar and syrup in a microwave-safe bowl and cook on HIGH for 1–2 minutes or until the butter has melted. Stir in the oats, cranberries and seeds and mix thoroughly. Press into a small greased or baking paper-lined microwave-safe baking dish. Cook on HIGH for about 5 minutes or until the centre is bubbling.
Makes 9 or 12 bars

chocolate chip biscuits

see variations page 279

Some foods deserve their reputation and this is one of them. If you are going to master any biscuit, let it be this one. The crunchy nuts and soft chocolate make these irresistible, especially with a glass of ice-cold milk. The dough can be stored, covered, in the fridge for up to five days, so you can have fresh biscuits whenever you want.

50 g (2 oz) butter, at room temperature
50 g (2 oz) caster sugar
50 g (2 oz) brown sugar
1 egg, lightly beaten
½ tsp vanilla extract

150 g (5 oz) self-raising flour, sifted
175 g (6 oz) chocolate chips
65 g (2½ oz) chopped pecans

Preheat the oven to 190ºC (Gas Mark 5). Grease a baking sheet with a little oil or butter or line with baking parchment.

In a large mixing bowl and using a wooden spoon, beat together the butter and caster and brown sugars until soft and fluffy (this will take about 5 minutes by hand). Add the egg and beat well to combine, then stir in the vanilla extract. Now gently fold the sifted flour into the batter with a metal spoon or spatula, taking care not to lose all the lightness you have beaten into the batter. Carefully fold in the chocolate chips and nuts.

Using a rounded teaspoon, drop the mixture onto the prepared baking sheet, leaving room between the rounds to allow them to spread while they cook. Bake for 8–10 minutes. Unless

you have several baking sheets, you will have to cook them in batches. If you want larger biscuits, use a rounded tablespoon and cook for a couple of minutes longer.

Makes about 30 x 5 cm (2 in) biscuits

moist banana muffins

see variations page 280

The natural sweetness and moisture in bananas means that you can reduce the sugar in these muffins without noticing. They can be made healthier still by using wholemeal flour, as shown in the variations. Unfortunately, you can't get away without buying a muffin tin, but as you always use paper muffin cases for making muffins, you don't have to buy an expensive one.

225 g (8 oz) plain flour
1 tsp bicarbonate of soda
½ tsp baking powder
½ tsp salt

3 large ripe bananas, mashed
225 g (8 oz) caster sugar
1 egg
60 g (2½ oz) butter, melted

Preheat the oven to 175ºC (Gas Mark 4). Put 12 muffin paper cases into the recesses of a 12-cup muffin tin.

Sift together the flour, bicarbonate of soda, baking powder and salt and set aside.

In a large bowl, combine the banana, sugar, egg and melted butter. Fold in the flour mixture and mix until the ingredients are combined but the batter is still slightly lumpy; do not over-mix or the muffins will be heavy. Spoon evenly into the paper cases in the muffin tin.

Bake for 25–30 minutes or until the muffins are well risen and spring back when lightly tapped. Cool for 5 minutes, then turn out onto a wire rack to cool completely.

Makes 12

cinnamon palmiers

see variations page 281

Palmiers look really impressive but are deceptively simple to make. This version is a quick and easy variation of the French classic. Serve at the end of a meal or take them to friends' when you are invited for dinner.

1 sheet of puff pastry, thawed
3 tbsp brown sugar

1 tsp ground cinnamon
flour, for dusting

Preheat the oven to 220°C (Gas Mark 7). Grease 1 or 2 baking sheets with oil or line them with baking paper.

Put the pastry on a floured surface. Sprinkle 2 tablespoons of brown sugar over the surface of the pastry, then dust with two-thirds of the cinnamon. Fold each of the short sides of the pastry into the centre; press down and sprinkle over the remaining sugar and cinnamon. Again, fold each pastry side in half so that they meet in the centre. Brush the pastry with cold water and fold over to make a long roll.

Cut across the roll to make roughly 5 mm (¼ in) slices (this is best done with a serrated knife), then transfer the slices to the baking sheet, leaving 2.5 cm (1 in) between each one to allow room for spreading.

Bake for about 10 minutes until golden. Remove from the baking sheet with a metal spatula and cool on a wire rack. These are best eaten on the day they are made, when they are really crisp, but will store for a few days in an airtight container.
Makes 18–20

tiffin

see variations page 282

A recipe for nervous bakers – all you have to do is melt the chocolate and sugar and crush a few biscuits and you have a cake you can be proud of! Beware – these biscuits are extremely high in calories, so don't make them too often and do share them!

100 g (3½ oz) butter or hard margarine
   (low-fat soft margarine will not set)
2 tbsp light brown sugar
4 tbsp cocoa powder

4 tbsp golden syrup
175 g (6 oz) digestive biscuits, crushed
65 g (2½ oz) raisins
4 tbsp dried cranberries

In a saucepan over a medium-low heat, melt together the butter, sugar, cocoa powder and syrup until the sugar crystals have disappeared. Stir in the crushed biscuits, the raisins and the cranberries.

Line a 20 cm (8 in) square cake tin with clingfilm. Press the mixture into the tin and flatten the surface with the back of a spoon. Using the tip of a knife, mark the surface into squares, then leave to set in a cool place. Slice when cooled, using your score marks to guide you.

Note: you can add a topping made from 125 g (4 oz) melted plain chocolate, spread over the bars and set before slicing, if liked.

Makes 9 or 12 slices

coffee & walnut mug cake

see variations page 283

Mug cakes are becoming really popular – the idea of creating a one-person cake in a few minutes is almost irresistible.

2 tbsp melted butter
¼ tsp instant coffee
½ tsp warm water
2 tbsp caster sugar or brown sugar
2 tbsp beaten egg (about ½ egg)
2 tbsp plain flour
¼ tsp baking powder
3 walnut halves, finely chopped

icing
¼ tsp instant coffee
¼ tsp warm water
1½ tsp butter, at room temperature
1½ tbsp icing sugar, sifted
walnut piece, for decoration

Select a mug with a capacity of 225–300 ml (8–10 fl oz). Put the butter in the mug and melt it in the microwave on HIGH for 20–30 seconds. Carefully swirl the butter around the inside of the mug to grease the sides.

To make the cake mixture, dissolve the instant coffee in the water, then add the coffee to the melted butter in the mug. Add all of the remaining ingredients and beat the mixture to a smooth batter using a fork. Put the mug back into the microwave and cook on HIGH for 1 minute and 20 seconds. Leave the mug to stand in the microwave without opening the door for 1 minute. Allow to cool. If liked, you can remove the cake from the mug after 5 minutes and continue to cool on a wire rack.

To make the icing, dissolve the instant coffee in the water, then beat all the ingredients together with a fork until the mixture is smooth. Use to decorate the cooled cake and top with a piece of walnut.

Note: microwave times may vary slightly. Add an additional 20–30 seconds for a machine under 1000 watts.

Makes 1

variations

fudgy brownies

see base recipe page 263

nutty brownies
After adding the flour, stir in 65 g (2½ oz) chopped nuts. Try pecans, walnuts, macadamia or mixed nuts – they all work well.

peanut butter brownies
Stir in 2 tablespoons peanut butter with the vanilla and 4 tablespoons chopped unsalted peanuts after the flour.

marshmallow brownies
Stir in 50 g (2 oz) mini marshmallows after the flour.

double chocolate brownies
Stir in 75 g (3 oz) white chocolate chips after the flour. Or use a selection of white, milk and plain chocolate chips.

variations

vanilla birthday cake

see base recipe page 264

vanilla cake with chocolate icing
Replace the vanilla icing with chocolate icing. Mix 50 g (2 oz) melted and cooled plain
chocolate into the butter, then stir into the sugar. Reduce the vanilla to 1 teaspoon.

vanilla cake with cream & strawberries
Beat 350 ml (12 fl oz) cream until thickened; sweeten to taste with 2–4 tablespoons sifted
icing sugar and stir in a few drops of vanilla extract. Spread half the cream over the cake.
Add a layer of sliced strawberries. Top with the other cake and repeat. You'll need about
225 g (8 oz) strawberries for the filling.

chocolate cake with vanilla icing
When making the cake, replace 4 tablespoons of the flour with 4 tablespoons sifted cocoa
powder. This is good with the chocolate icing too.

orange cake
Replace the vanilla with the grated zest of 1 orange. Squeeze the juice of the orange into
a measuring jug and add enough milk to yield 150 ml (¼ pint) of liquid. For the icing, use
1 teaspoon grated orange zest and replace the milk with orange juice; omit the vanilla.

vanilla cupcakes
Put paper cupcake cases in a muffin tin. Half-fill each case with the batter; bake for
20 minutes. Decorate with the icing when cooled. Makes about 18.

variations

cranberry flapjacks

see base recipe page 267

chocolate-coated flapjacks

Melt 125 g (4 oz) plain chocolate in the microwave on HIGH in short 20-second intervals, stirring between each interval, until melted and smooth. Pour the melted chocolate over the cooled flapjacks. When the chocolate is partially set, score the top of the flapjacks into squares to make slicing easier.

raisin & pecan flapjacks

Replace the cranberries with raisins and replace the pumpkin seeds with chopped pecans.

sour cherry coconut flapjacks

Replace the cranberries and pumpkin seeds with 20 g (2 oz) desiccated coconut and 4 tablespoons chopped sour cherries.

ginger flapjacks

Add 2 teaspoons ground ginger to the mixture. Replace the cranberries with chopped crystallised ginger.

variations

chocolate chip biscuits

see base recipe page 268

triple chocolate chip biscuits
Add 2 tablespoons cocoa powder into the flour mixture. Use 75 g (3 oz) each of plain chocolate chips and white chocolate chips.

raisin & orange biscuits
Replace the chocolate chips with 150 g (5 oz) raisins. Reduce the vanilla to ¼ teaspoon and add the grated zest of 1 orange into the mixture with the vanilla.

granola biscuits
Replace the chocolate chips and nuts with 100 g (3½ oz) granola or muesli.

chocolate chip cookie bars
Preheat the oven to 175ºC (Gas Mark 4). Line a 20 x 20 cm (8 x 8 in) cake tin with baking paper and grease the sides of the tin. Make the dough as directed and spread it into the prepared tin. Bake for 20–30 minutes until golden brown – a wooden cocktail stick inserted into the centre should come out clean. Do not over-bake. Cool on a wire rack then cut into 9 or 12 bars and remove from the tin to cool completely.

variations

moist banana muffins

see base recipe page 270

chunky whole food banana muffins
Use only 50 g (2 oz) plain flour and add 50 g (2 oz) plain wholemeal flour. Mash 2 bananas and chop the third into small pieces.

cinnamon banana nut muffins
Sift 1 teaspoon ground cinnamon in with the flour. Stir 75 g (3 oz) chopped pecans, walnuts or mixed nuts into the mixture with the other ingredients.

banana chocolate chip muffins
Stir 75 g (3 oz) plain chocolate chips into the mixture with the other ingredients.

banana crunch muffins
Mix 3 tablespoons granola into the mixture with the other ingredients.

variations

cinnamon palmiers

see base recipe page 271

nutella palmiers
Omit the sugar and cinnamon and spread the pastry with a thin layer of Nutella or other chocolate paste (about 6 tablespoons).

raspberry & orange palmiers
Omit the sugar and cinnamon and spread the pastry with a thin layer of raspberry jam (about 6 tablespoons) and the grated zest of ½ orange.

pesto palmiers
Omit the sugar and cinnamon and spread the pastry with a thin layer of pesto (about 6 tablespoons) and 2 tablespoons grated Parmesan cheese.

parmesan oliver twists
Omit the sugar and cinnamon and spread the pastry with a thin layer of tapenade, (about 6 tablespoons) and 2 tablespoons grated Parmesan cheese.

tiffin

see base recipe page 273

rocky road slice
Follow the basic recipe but omit the raisins and cranberries. Replace with 3 tablespoons each of mini marshmallows, white chocolate chips and unsalted peanut halves.

two-chocolate macadamia slice
Follow the basic recipe but omit the raisins. Replace with 75 g (3 oz) each of white chocolate chips and chopped macadamia nuts.

chocolate cherry slice
Follow the basic recipe but omit the raisins. Replace with 50 g (2 oz) dried sour cherries and 75 g (3 oz) flaked almonds.

chocolate, coconut & cranberry slice
Follow the basic recipe but omit the raisins. Replace with 40 g (1½ oz) desiccated coconut and 100 g (3½ oz) dried cranberries.

coffee & walnut mug cake

see base recipe page 274

coffee & chocolate chip mug cake
Replace the walnuts with 2 tablespoons plain chocolate chips.

mocha mug cake
Replace the walnuts with ½ teaspoon cocoa powder. Decorate the cake with little chocolates.

lemon drizzle mug cake
Omit the coffee and water. Add ¼ teaspoon grated lemon zest and 1 teaspoon lemon juice to the cake batter. Replace the icing with a drizzle made from 1 teaspoon sugar mixed with 1 teaspoon lemon juice. Drizzle this over the cake while still warm.

chocolate walnut mug cake
Omit the coffee and water from both the cake and the icing. Add 1 teaspoon cocoa powder with the other cake ingredients. Add ½ tablespoon melted chocolate chips to the icing.

index